Life After Early Retirement

Life After Early Retirement

The Experiences of
Lower-Level Workers

Dean W. Morse
Anna B. Dutka
Susan H. Gray

Foreword by Eli Ginzberg

LandMark Studies
ROWMAN & ALLANHELD *Publishers*

ROWMAN & ALLANHELD

Published in the United States of America in 1983
by Rowman & Allanheld, Publishers
(A Division of Littlefield, Adams & Company)
81 Adams Drive, Totowa, New Jersey 07512

Library of Congress Cataloging in Publication Data

Morse, Dean.
  Life after early retirement.

  (Conservation of human resources series ; 17)
  Includes bibliographical references and index.
  1. Retirement—United States. 2. Labor and laboring
classes—United States. 3. White collar workers—
United States. I. Dutka, Anna B. II. Gray, Susan H.
III. Title. IV. Series.
HQ1064.U5M683 1983   306′.38   81–70970
ISBN 0–916672–62–X

The survey that provided the data utilized in this book was funded
by the Employment and Training Administration, U.S. Department of Labor, under research and development grant No. USDL
21-36-79-25. Since grantees conducting research and development
projects under government sponsorship are encouraged to express
their own judgment freely, this book, although assisted by the Department of Labor, does not necessarily represent the official opinion or policy of the Department of Labor. The grantee is solely responsible for the contents of this book.

83 84 85 86 / 10 9 8 7 6 5 4 3 2 1

*Dedicated to our Respondents
who shared with us both the disappointments
and gratifications of early retirement and
pointed the way to improved policy.*

Table of Contents

Tables   ix
Foreword by Eli Ginzberg   xi

Chapters
1   Introduction   1
2   The Retirement Decision   17
3   Postretirement Work Experience   34
4   Unpaid Activities   53
5   Life After Retirement: Successes, Disappointments, and Reactions   63
6   What Difference Did Gender Make? Or the Company One Kept?   81
7   The Retirement Experience of Major Subgroups   100
8   The Retirement of Male Nonsupervisory Personnel Compared with Managerial, Professional, and Technical Personnel   120
9   Retirement: Change and Continuity   131

Appendices
A   Retirement Activities Study Questionnaire   148
B   Percentage Distributions: Single-Response Questions   162
C   Percentage Distributions: Multi-Response Questions   172
D   Selected Cross-Tabulations   179
E   Statistical Models of the Retirement Decision and the Decision to Work in Retirement   184

Index   191

List of Tables

1.1 Labor Force Participation Rates of Selected White
 Male and Female Age Groups: 1950–1980   2

1.2 Preretirement Job Classification by Skill Level and
 Training Requirements   11

2.1 Preretirement Plans, by Area   25

2.2 Employment During Retirement by Retirement
 Expectations   31

3.1 Reasons Given for Postretirement Work   35

3.2 Hourly Wage Rates of the "Currently Employed"   42

4.1 Time Spent in Hobbies and Recreational Activities
 Before Retirement and in Last 12 Months   57

5.1 Problems Encountered Postretirement   65

5.2 Interaction Among Problems: Cross-Tabulation of
 Major Problems Encountered During Retirement
 by Major Problems Encountered During
 Retirement   74

5.3 Possible Changes in Retirement Timing   78

5.4 Summary: Possible Changes in Retirement Timing   79

6.1 Reasons for Early Retirment by Sex and Company,
 Responses as Percentage of Respondents   92

7.1 Actual Health, Income, and Social Life Compared
 with Preretirement Expectations by Vintages I
 and II   103

7.2 Percentage of Respondents in Vintages I and II
 Who Encountered Selected Problems During
 Retirement   103

7.3   Age of Vintages I and II at Time of Survey   105

7.4   Age at Retirement (by company)   111

7.5   Age at Retirement by Five Vintages of Year of
Retirement, Grouped   112

7.6   Reasons for Retirement by Selected Age Group   113

7.7   Work Experience and Work Status at Time of
Survey by Age Group at Retirement   116

7.8   Work Experience and Employment Status at Time
of Survey by Age Group at Time of Survey   117

8.1   Major Reasons for Retirement: MTP and NS
Respondents   123

8.2   Work Experience of Managerial, Professional, and
Technical Personnel and Male Nonsupervisory
Personnel during Retirement   125

8.3   Percentage Distribution of MPT Respondents and
Male NS Respondents by Amount of Time Spent
per Week in Major Activity Areas   129

Foreword

Research is a process in which what is learned from one investigation often becomes the jumping-off place for the next exploration. This is surely the case with the present inquiry, which follows an earlier study of early retirement that was focused on the same three companies, a manufacturer, a utility, and a retailer—all major U.S. corporations. The time period—the decade of the late 1960s to the late 1970s—is also the same. But there are two important differences: one planned, the other a concomitant of the selection process.

The first study, published in a volume entitled *Early Retirement: Boon or Bane?*, focused on the middle managers and technical personnel whose earnings at the time of retirement fell in the $20,000 to $50,000 range. The second study herein reported focused on nonsupervisory personnel, that is, on skilled and semiskilled blue-collar workers and on the lower levels of sales, clerical, and service personnel—individuals who on the average earned less than $8 an hour (in 1979 dollars) at the time of their retirement and whose family incomes amounted to approximately $22,000.

The second important difference that emerged was the fact that women represented just under half of the entire group covered by the present study, while they had accounted for no more than 5 percent in the first investigation.

Both the managerial and the nonsupervisory studies were drawn from the retired personnel of the same companies under specifications set by the Conservation of Human Resources. The basic instrument in each case was a mailed questionnaire; while 70 percent of the managerial personnel responded, the rate of response of the nonsupervisory group, who provided the material for the present investigation, was about 50 percent. In both instances, many of the respondents availed themselves of the opportunity to expand on their answers by writing freely about their feelings concerning retirement.

The Statistical Overview that forms the first section of the introduction covers most of the salient facts that the investigators have extracted from their systematic analysis of the replies. It is therefore not necessary for me to go over the same ground here. Rather, I will draw attention to a limited number of findings that impressed me because of their import for public policy with respect to retirement. At the beginning of 1982, U.S. workers' thinking on retirement is clearly in a state of flux.

The mean age of retirement of the nonsupervisory group was 60.5 years. This underscores the extent to which a significant proportion of American workers opt for early retirement, even before they become eligible for reduced Social Security benefits. Small wonder, therefore, that the Reagan administration's proposal to cut back drastically the amount of benefits available to early retirees between ages 62 and 65 failed to attract a single supporting vote in the U.S. Senate.

Whatever academicians, physicians, moralists, and other proponents may believe about the virtues of work and the desirability of persons capable of working to continue to do so into their late sixties and even seventies, those workers who responded to our questionnaire do not agree. For the most part they retired early of their own free will and, what is more, most of them are convinced, in retrospect, that they had made the right decision. They expected their retirement years to be satisfying, and they report that on balance their retirement has been just that.

As one examines more closely the reasons why the respondents retired early, one finds an admixture of both positive and negative factors: some reported that they could afford to retire and/or they had worked long enough; some reported that their health was poor and/or they were under pressure from their superiors or fellow workers to retire. While one in four had worked part time or full time after retirement, only one in eight continued in the workforce as fully attached workers. Most respondents were apparently glad to leave the world of work behind them.

Several additional findings about work merit at least brief comment. About one in four who didn't work after retirement explained that it did not pay them to take a job. On the other hand, many who did work were willing to accept a job in a field different from the one in which they had been previously employed, although it paid considerably less and offered few if any fringe benefits. Despite these negatives, they reported that they enjoyed what they were doing. In fact, they liked their present job better than the one they held prior to retirement.

Another interesting comment about working after retirement is that more than half the group indicated that they might "consider" working at some time in the future. The final comment relates to the importance of social factors in working: many sought companionship more than money in going back to work.

It is probably not stretching matters too far to say that the prospect of these early retirees working in the future is related to the unease that many reported about "inflation," which, more than any other factor, had muddied the waters between their expectations about retirement and their actual experiences. While most expected their retirement years to be satisfactory and so they had turned out to be, inflation had created problems that many had not foreseen and that had made their coping difficult.

We know much less about women who have worked regularly and then retire than about men. The present study helps to fill in some of the gaps. Among the striking facts that emerge is that the women workers on average earned only 60 percent of male earnings, and since only one in two women, in contrast to nine out of ten of the men, were married at the time of the survey, their family as well as their personal income was much lower. Those who returned to work did so, even more than in the case of men, for "social reasons."

I have recently dealt at length with Social Security in the United States.* In that article I pointed out that there is little prospect of stabilizing the long-term finances of the system unless we begin in the immediate future to raise the retirement age from 65 to 68; that such a change might need to make allowance for the earlier retirement of those who have worked long years in physically demanding jobs. But many of the respondents in this study would not fall into such a special category, since their work has not been physically demanding. Accordingly, we confront workers who opted to leave the workforce at around 60 with a policy recommendation

---

*"The Social Security System," *Scientific American*, January 1982.

that 68 should be the new target figure. The reconciliation of such conflicting priorities presents a major challenge. We need to study the findings in this volume, and we need to undertake additional studies that broaden and deepen our insights into people's capacities, expectations, and responses to all aspects of retirement if we are to redesign our national policies intelligently. Fiscal integrity is critically important, but only if the Social Security system seems responsive to other high-priority goals of the American people.

For reasons of confidentiality I am unable to identify by name the three major American corporations whose interest and help made this study possible. Similarly, I can merely express our appreciation in general to the respondents whose replies provided the basic material for the analysis and findings. But I am pleased to be able to acknowledge our indebtedness to the U.S. Department of Labor, Office of Research and Development, which provided the funding for this research.

Finally, the authors join me in expressing appreciation to Shoshana Vasheetz for her invaluable contribution to the production of this volume.

Eli Ginzberg, Director
Conservation of Human Resources
Columbia University

CHAPTER 1
Introduction

In the first part of a study of the retirement experiences of individuals who retired between 1968 and 1978 from three large American corporations, the experiences of middle-level managerial, professional, and technical personnel were the subject of the investigation published in 1980 under the title *Early Retirement: Boon or Bane?* The present investigation of nonsupervisory personnel focuses upon many of the same questions raised with the first group, but with the questionnaire instrument having been somewhat altered to take account of the differences between the two groups of respondents.

The three companies—a large manufacturer, a chain store, and a utility, all with multiple establishments throughout the nation—provided us with panels of retired nonsupervisory personnel who were distributed equally with respect to year of retirement between 1968 and 1978. One-fifth had been mandatorily retired and the others had taken early retirement voluntarily.

A PROFILE OF RESPONDENTS

Slightly more than half the respondents (54%) were men.* The mean age of respondents at retirement was 60.5 years, after an av-

---

*The interested reader will find in Appendices A through D the survey instrument and percentage distributions of respondents by their answers to single-response and multi-response questions.

erage of 27 years work with the company from which they retired.
While almost evenly divided by sex, they were overwhelmingly—
about 99 percent—white. Two out of five had less than a high
school education; one out of ten, less than nine years of education;
two out of five, a high school degree. One out of five had some
college education, but only one out of fifty had a college degree.
When they retired, approximately three out of four were married,
one out of eight was widowed, one out of six was either divorced or
separated, and one out of fourteen had never married. At the time
of the survey, almost one out of five was widowed.

In 1979 dollars, the mean hourly earnings before retirement of
the respondents was $7.79; their mean total family income before
retirement was $22,260. Since the three companies from which
they retired, hereafter referred to as "Utility," "Manufacturer,"
and "Chain Store," were very different in character, the diversity of
the respondents by occupation and skill level was large. Respondents were assigned to job categories on the basis of their descriptions of their actual jobs at the time of their retirement. The diversity of their work is of course far greater than can be suggested by a
summary table that emphasizes skill and whether a job was white
collar or blue collar in character. Nevertheless, we have classified
them as shown in Table 1.1.

One-sixth of our respondents reported that their preretirement
work involved supervisory or administrative activities. It should be
noted that while they were not classified by their companies as
managers, many nonsupervisory employees were actually engaged,
at least in part, in such activities. Another sixth of the respondents
was composed of three groups: (a) technical, clerical, and service
workers whose occupations required at least three months of training before their employment, (b) high-skilled white-collar employees, and (c) high-skilled blue-collar employees. About three out of
ten of the respondents were engaged in skilled and semiskilled occupations. Low-skilled clerical or sales workers comprised about a
quarter of the respondents, while low-skilled blue-collar workers
accounted for about one out of eight of the respondents. The distribution of hourly wage rates and total family income, adjusted to
1979 dollars, reflected the wide diversity in skill and type of occupation and work responsibility.

Finally, the mean age of the respondents at the time of the survey was about 67. Their age distribution at that time was as follows:

Respondents' ages at time of survey	Percentage of respondents
50-54	1
55-59	7
60-64	19
65-69	40
70-74	28
75 and older	5
Total	100

OVERVIEW OF RESPONSES

The Retirement Decision: Reasons for Retirement

Twenty-four percent of our respondents reported that they had retired because of mandatory retirement policies of their companies. This is a slightly higher percentage than would have been expected if the respondents had been randomly drawn from the panels drawn by their companies from their retired employees and if that panel was drawn in accordance with the provision that one-fifth of it be composed of mandatorily retired employees.*

The remainder of the respondents reported that they had retired before reaching mandatory age. These early retirees gave four major nonexclusive reasons for their retirement, in each case about two out of five indicating that the reason contributed to their decision. The four reasons were (a) they could afford retirement, (b) their health made it necessary or desirable, (c) they had worked long enough, and (d) pressures of their work or treatment of older workers induced their retirement.

Two other reasons were given, but much less frequently. One-sixth of the early retirees indicated that the receipt of disability benefits, either from Social Security or from their company benefit systems, contributed to their retirement decision. About one out of eight of the respondents reported that one of the reasons for their retirement was their feeling that it did not pay to work any longer; about one out of twenty said that a supervisor had suggested retirement.

Four out of five of the respondents reported that in retrospect they retired at about the right time, almost all the rest that they had

---

*A few respondents who had retired before age 62 classified themselves as "mandatorily" retired.

Table 1.1 Preretirement Job Classification by Skill Level
          and Training Requirements

Job classification	Percentage of respondents	
High-skill white collar	2	10
High-skill blue collar	8	
Other skilled and semiskilled white and blue collar occupations (requiring from 3 months to two years training)	30	30
Low-skill clerical and sales	26	39
Low-skill blue collar	12	
Low-skill service	1	
Managers, administrators and supervisors, self-classified	15	15
Technical, clerical and service workers, preemployment training of at least 3 months	6	6
Total	100	100

Note: Training routes for these occupations vary widely and
      pay scales are quite dissimilar. The reader inter-
      ested in the general rationale of the system of job
      classification we have used is referred to Marcia
      Freedman and Anna B. Dutka, Training Information for
      Policy Guidance. R&D Monograph 76. (U.S. Department
      of Labor, ETA, 1980).

retired too soon. At the time of their retirement nine out of ten of
the respondents expected that their retirement would be a pleasant
experience, almost two-thirds of the respondents reporting that
they had looked forward to a "very pleasant" retirement.

Half the respondents knew at least a year in advance when they
would retire. Another quarter reported that they knew at least
three months in advance, but less than a year. One in seven reported that retirement came as a surprise, and one in eight that
they had less than three months foreknowledge.

Even though about a quarter of the respondents had little or no advance knowledge of when they would retire, almost all the respondents reported at least some planning for retirement (not knowing the exact date of retirement does not prevent some kinds of contingent planning about certain aspects of retirement). Only one in eight planned to work during the retirement years. About one in six reported an intention to move to a new residential location. Most of the other types of planning centered upon how to use time, for example in such areas as home maintenance, new and old hobbies, and so forth. Most of the respondents indicated that planning was useful, and almost one-half stated that it was very useful.

About one-half of the respondents had received some form of guidance or counseling from their companies; one-sixth, however, reported receiving "very little" in the way of preretirement guidance or counseling; a third said that they had received none at all. A third of the respondents felt that it would have been desirable to have received more of these preretirement services, two out of five that they were satisfied with the amount they had received, while about a quarter reported that they did not think that such services were useful.

Useful information about retirement came from a number of sources, but the respondents indicated that their companies were much more likely to be such a source than friends and relatives—three out of five reporting companies as a source, only one out of five reporting friends and relatives. Apparently the latter do not usually possess the kinds of information that help an individual make a decision to retire or plan for retirement itself. Company programs to provide such information clearly have a wide audience, but even so, about two out of five of the respondents did not name their company as a source. About one quarter of the respondents said that they had received *no* useful information about retirement from any source.

Postretirement Problems

Although they had expected that retirement would be pleasant and generally reported that these expectations were more or less confirmed by their actual experience, respondents did report that they had encountered several serious problems during retirement. The most frequently mentioned of these was inflation. Nine out of ten considered it to be a problem, and two out of three reported it as one of the three most serious problems encountered. Almost two out of five mentioned their health as a problem. Slightly more than a quarter of the respondents reported that it was one of the three most serious problems; spouse's health was considered a serious problem almost as frequently.

Far fewer respondents reported problems related to feelings of uselessness, boredom, or lack of contact with friends and family. Instead, they reported such problems as lack of personal security (one out of six) and inadequate transportation (one out of six).

Postretirement Work

Many of the respondents indicated that economic pressures had forced them to make radical adjustments in their standard of living, and for some, this adjustment included working during retirement. Somewhat to our surprise, however, the reasons given for working during retirement were more apt to be social than economic. Almost a quarter of the respondents had some type of work experience during retirement, and about one-eighth indicated that they had worked most, if not almost all, of the months of their retirement. About one in eight of the respondents was employed at the time of the survey, and about one-sixth of them reported they were either employed at the time of the survey or had been employed at some time during the 12 months preceding the survey.

Although, or perhaps because, the respondents had worked before retirement for three of the largest companies in the United States, their employers in retirement were much more likely to be small companies. About half of the respondents who worked for a company during retirement worked for one with fewer than fifty employees. Only about one in eight worked for a company that employed more than a thousand people. Finally, about a third of the respondents who reported work experience during retirement were either self-employed or were employed by a private individual.

The great majority of respondents, almost four out of five, who reported employment during retirement said that they obtained their jobs either immediately or within a month. Only a handful reported an unsuccessful job search. Jobs were obtained primarily through friends, relatives, or other contacts, or by direct application to employers. Almost none got jobs by means of either private or public employment agencies. About one-fifth said that they got jobs through want ads.

Although respondents who obtained jobs reported little or no difficulty in finding employment, another group of respondents did report such difficulty. These were the almost sixty respondents who, when asked why they had never worked during retirement, reported that they did not think that there were any suitable jobs either in their own field or in any field. It seems evident, however, that many of the respondents who said that there were no suitable jobs did not in fact make an intensive search for employment. It is more likely that these respondents reflected the general sense of their associates and their community that suitable jobs were not available to retired people, and therefore did not actively search for employment. It is worth noting that, if all of those respondents who believed that no suitable jobs were available to them had actually worked at some time during retirement, the rate of work experience among the respondents as a whole would have risen from about 24 percent to about 30 percent.

Among the reasons given for not wanting to work during retirement, three stood out vividly from the rest. About a third of the respondents reported that their health status prevented working. About one-half reported that they simply did not want to work. But more than a quarter of them reported that among the reasons they did not work during retirement was the fact that it did not pay to work. Two developments might alter the decision of this last group not to work. The first would be any factor that changed their perceptions about the net return from paid work, including a reduction or elimination of the Social Security penalty for earnings above a fixed cut-off. The second would be anything that increased the severity of pressures upon their present economic resources— particularly inflation, but also such pressures as the cost of catastrophic illness and increasing anxiety about future sources of income.

About one-half of those who reported work experience during retirement worked during all or almost all months or most months, and these respondents were very likely to be working at the time of the survey. In other words, about an eighth of the respondents formed a group who were committed to more or less continual work during their retirement. Moreover, almost all these respondents had worked for no more than one or two employers during the course of their retirement years.

The kind of work respondents did after retirement usually differed from the work they did prior to retirement, two-thirds of them reporting in fact that it was very different. But this did not prevent many of them from deriving satisfaction from their postretirement work. In fact, for many the fact that their work was different was in itself a positive source of satisfaction. A third of the respondents who worked during retirement said that their work was more satisfying than what they had done before retiring. Only a fifth said that it was less satisfactory.

A noteworthy characteristic of postretirement work experience was that for a sizeable minority it usually involved relatively full-time, full-year work. About one-sixth of the respondents with work experience reported that they customarily worked at least 35 hours a week and 48 weeks a year. About three out of five worked at least 20 hours a week and 20 weeks a year. Only about one-seventh reported that they customarily worked less than 20 hours a week and 20 weeks a year. While there was great diversity in actual work schedules, by hours per week and weeks per year, respondents generally indicated that their actual work schedules were close to what they preferred.

Although most respondents, almost four out of five, reported that they were at least as satisfied with their postretirement jobs as they were with their preretirement work activity, this was not because these postretirement jobs paid well. Quite the contrary. For the majority, postretirement work meant a drastic reduction in hourly pay and fringe benefits. Almost three out of five reported that their hourly pay was either less than or not more than half of what they earned before retirement. Seventy percent reported no fringe benefits; another 16 percent reported that fringe benefits were "much less" than preretirement benefits.

The fact that almost a quarter of the respondents who did not work during retirement said that the reason they did not work was that "it does not pay" is vividly confirmed by the actual hourly pay and fringe benefits received by the great majority of the respondents who did work during retirement. Since American workers are quite reluctant to accept jobs with a reduction in pay or that represent a reduction in status, the fact that almost a quarter of the respondents did work in spite of the fact that they had to accept a radical reduction in pay (and probably in status too) is noteworthy. It also indicates that a much higher proportion of the respondents might have worked if postretirement work were not associated in their minds with radical reductions in pay and status.

Seven out of ten of those respondents who worked in spite of relatively low hourly pay rates and little or no fringe benefits reported they were "happy to discover that their skills and experience have been appreciated and respected." More than half of them also said that they were happy to work because they were able to do things at work which they could not do before they retired.

Respondents were asked questions about their involvement in nonwork activities as well as about their postretirement work experience. About a third said that they engaged in volunteer work, but the hours spent in such activity were usually very modest. Only one in twenty spent at least ten hours a week in volunteer work. The great majority of respondents also reported being engaged in hobbies or spending some time in recreational activities, but the range of reported hours per week was very large. Modest amounts of time (ten hours or less) were reported by one-half of those who responded to this question.

The pattern of hours spent on domestic chores was quite similar to that spent on hobbies and recreational activities. A somewhat smaller number of respondents, about six out of ten, reported spending time on home maintenance. Nonetheless, about one in eight reported spending a considerable amount of time, ten hours a week or more, in this activity.

Very few respondents indicated that they spent little or no time in any of these activities. What does seem to stand out is that the amount of time spent in nonwork activities is not correlated to any degree with the amount of time devoted to paid work. There is no clear-cut evidence that respondents substituted work for the nonwork activities. Low levels of activity in nonwork areas was most clearly related to health status, either of the respondent or of the respondent's spouse; but even in the case of those respondents who reported health problems, a significant proportion maintained relatively high levels of activity, both in the form of paid work and in unpaid activities. Many respondents in their written comments took pains to emphasize that they kept active in spite of health limitations in the belief that activity made their situation more tolerable or prevented their health from deteriorating further.

In addition to being asked how much time they typically spent on five major areas of activities, respondents were asked how often they had engaged in a wide range of specific recreational activities before they retired and in the year before the survey. The recreational activities ranged from active physical pursuits to passive recreational activities. In general, the striking finding that emerges from their responses to these questions is the extent to which activity levels were usually maintained, and even increased in some cases. There is little evidence in the responses of what might be called disengagement from activity, again excepting some, but not all, of those respondents who reported serious health problems. Where respondents were able physically to maintain a regimen of recreational activities, they seem generally to have continued the pattern that had characterized their preretirement recreational life, including such activities as active sports, gardening, travel, and the like.

While health status has been emphasized both as a critical factor in the retirement decisions of many respondents and as an important element in decisions to engage in postretirement activities, including work, it should be kept in mind that most of the respondents felt that their health was at least as good as that of the retired people of their own age. Two out of five in fact said that their health was better, and only one out of ten reported worse health. Our respondents therefore perceived themselves to be relatively well off with respect to health, were generally quite or very satisfied with their retirement, generally maintained relatively high levels of nonwork activity in comparison to their preretirement patterns, but at the same time felt anxious about, or threatened by, a number of actual and potential problems.

Although the great majority—three-quarters—have not worked after retirement, there is some evidence that this proportion might change substantially if economic pressures increase or if the rewards of paid work for retired individuals increase. Slightly more than half the respondents indicated that they might consider work at some time in the future. In other words, for every respondent who had some work experience in retirement, another respondent might be induced by a combination of pressures and incentives to reenter the labor market in the future.

Moreover, a considerable number of respondents indicated that a combination of company and national policies might have induced them to retire later than they actually did. Significantly, a smaller proportion indicated that they might have been induced to retire earlier. Two hundred and fifty of the respondents, almost a third, indicated that either one or more of a number of specific policies would have induced later retirement. Curiously, only one out of eight indicated that he or she would have retired later if mandatory retirement age had been 70. It will be recalled that almost one-quarter of the respondents reported that they had been mandatorily retired. Apparently only about half at most, of the mandatorily retired, would have retired later. What this seems to mean is that for many of the mandatorily retired, age 65 had become the age at which they believed that they *should* retire. In other words, a socially sanctioned norm seems to have become so strongly internalized that only half of these individuals who were mandatorily retired would have chosen to alter their behavior if the retirement age had been higher.

Age 65 as a retirement norm dates only from the late 19th century. Although the passage of a few decades was sufficient to make it the usual cut-off age for the majority of the U.S. population, it is clear that this norm has been eroded for a significant part of the population who have recently elected to retire earlier than age 65.

Table 1.2 Labor Force Participation Rates of Selected
White Male and Female Age Groups: 1950-1980

	45-54		55-64		65 and older	
	Male	Female	Male	Female	Male	Female
1950	96	36	87	26	46	9
1955	97	43	88	32	40	11
1960	96	49	87	36	33	11
1965	96	50	85	40	28	10
1970	95	54	83	43	27	10
1975	93	54	77	41	22	8
1980	92	60	74	42	19	8

Source: Employment and Training Report of the President,
1976 Table A-4, pp. 217-18 for 1950-1975; U.S.
Department of Labor, Bureau of Labor Statistics,
Employment and Earnings (April 1980), Table A-4,
pp. 23-24.

It is probable that the change in the age of legal mandatory retirement to 70 will erode this norm further or eliminate the very idea of any socially prescribed "correct" age for retirement.

The Problem of Retirement and Its Historical Setting

In the last few decades the phenomenon of early retirement has come increasingly to public attention. The implications of declining labor force participation on the part of older age groups has become, in the face of an aging population, a matter of serious concern not only to public officials, but also to the private sector in general and to many corporations. In part, the increase in early retirement is a natural response to liberalization of public and private benefit systems, which make it possible for older workers to afford to retire at an age earlier than what had previously been taken to be the norm.

That norm, age 65, was embodied in the original legislation that set up the Social Security Administration in the United States, and then was given further sanction by being included as the normal age of retirement in most private pension plans. Nevertheless, as Table 1.2 illustrates, labor force participation rates for each of the two older *male* age groups have steadily fallen since about 1950.

Only since 1965 has the labor force participation rate of white males aged 45 to 54 begun to fall, and the decline, though small, has continued. In contrast has been the rise in participation rates for white females, striking in the case of age group 45–54, but quite noticeable until 1970 in the case of women aged 55–64. Since 1970 the labor force participation rate of women in this age group has remained practically unchanged. Although the labor force participation rate for white males aged 55–64 has declined since 1960, much of this decline has been in the age group 60–64. The difference between labor force participation rates for white males aged 55–59 and 60–64 is now pronounced. In March 1980, 48 percent of those in the 55–59 group were in the labor force, but only 34 percent of those in the 60–64 age group.

Ages 62 and 65 represent important breakpoints in labor force participation rates. These of course are the ages at which workers covered by Social Security become eligible, first for reduced benefits and then for full benefits. Moreover, after age 65 there have been serious penalties for earning more than a relatively low amount, a penalty which amounts to a tax of 50 percent on each dollar earned, along with relatively small incentives in the form of increased Social Security benefits for additional years of work life and usually no increase in private pension benefits for delayed retirement. At the same time, many of the larger corporations have incorporated increasingly generous and liberal early retirement provisions in their company benefit plans, often with the strenuous urging of the unions that represent their workers.

From a historical viewpoint, this represents a watershed in human affairs and in the relationship between individuals and the world of work. Although a few countries, notably Germany, did institute Social Security systems in the 19th century which provided for retirement—in the case of Bismarck's Germany, first at age 70, later at age 65—such systems were usually confined to a limited segment of the labor force and to a population whose life expectancy was significantly lower than is the case in advanced industrial countries today. As a result, this is the first age of man in which it can be said, and this is true again only of the comparatively small number of countries which are among the advanced industrial countries of the world, that a socially significant portion of the population is retiring early enough to have several decades of more or less vigorous and healthy existence to look forward to (or to be anxious about, as the case may be).

At the very time that this phenomenon has come to public attention, a concomitant demographic development—the rapid decrease in birth rates that followed the high post-World War II birth rates—has created a potential crisis, expected to come to a head only in the first decades of the next century, in which increasing numbers of retired older workers will have to be supported by the productive efforts of a relatively decreasing number of active workers.

Although many factors may intervene to lessen or even eliminate this problem, it is still sufficiently imminent and probable to cause great concern, both among public and private officials charged with responsibility for developing policies with respect to retirement and postretirement benefit plans and among the public at large. The rapid decrease in confidence in the Social Security system's capacity to pay benefits to those covered by the system has reached critical proportions, especially among younger workers. A continued decline in this confidence threatens the social compact between generations upon which both public and private pension systems are necessarily based.

PERCEPTIONS OF AGING

From a different point of view, the increase in the absolute numbers of individuals who have retired with many remaining years of life raises questions about the effect of this long period of retirement upon them, and about the nature of the experiences and problems they encounter. Theories of aging are very much in flux. One theory, that of disengagement, was proposed, only to be countered by a theory of aging that emphasized the continuity of basic patterns of personality and activity levels. As one writer put it,

> The activity theory of aging assumes that older people are expected to continue to be active and to compensate for the loss of work or friends or spouse by increasing activities with other people. The self-concept, sources of satisfaction, and life style are not expected to change much. The rugged American individualist can survive aging by striving to wear out, not rust out.*

Detailed information about patterns of activity of individuals who have experienced early retirement, in contrast to those who have been mandatorily retired, can be expected to throw some light upon these and other theories of aging.

Meanwhile, in response to the increasing longevity of the popu-

---

*James W. Walker and Harriet L. Izer, *The End of Mandatory Retirement* (New York: John Wiley & Sons, 1978), p. 169.

lation and the heightened physical and mental well-being of individuals who are more than 60 years old, the aging portion of the population has been differentiated by gerontologists into at least two groups whose physical circumstances and problems are in general apt to be quite different. The first group is the young-old (60–75), the second the old-old (75+).

This recognition of gross differentiation between different parts of the aging portion of the population is mirrored by a heightened appreciation of the heterogeneity of the aging population. From a number of critical points of view, the older age groups of the population are more heterogenous than are the younger age groups. This is an inevitable part of the aging process itself, which exposes individuals who make up an age cohort to ceaseless developments that tend to differentiate them from their fellows. But it is also a result in part of the historical experience of that part of the U.S. population who are now in the older age groups. Some of the most striking events of the last century, including several wars, have left strong and indelible marks on part of the older population and not on the rest of it. As a result, the population of the United States now more than 60 years of age is extraordinarily diverse in its historical experiences.

How this diverse aging population reacts to retirement is therefore a matter of real moment to society in general and to policymakers in particular. Whatever lessons their present experiences can provide—to help succeeding generations of older individuals cope with the retirement process, and/or to recast retirement policies in more flexible and constructive forms—will be well worth learning.

The Retirement Activities Study

The investigation that is summed up in the following pages is part of an ongoing study, the first part of which, completed in 1979, reported the experiences of slightly more than one thousand managerial, professional and technical personnel.* Their mailed questionnaire queried their decision to retire, their planning for retirement, their expectations about retirement, their postretire-

---

*Dean W. Morse and Susan H. Gray, *Early Retirement—Boon or Bane?* (Montclair, N.J.: Allanheld, Osmun, 1980).

ment work experiences, and their other postretirement activities.

In addition, they were encouraged to write comments about national and company policies with respect to retirement and to comment upon the satisfactions and dissatisfactions of their retirement years. Seven out of ten individuals who were sent questionnaires responded, and more than half of the respondents provided written comments, often very extensive, about a host of retirement experiences and about public and private policies which affect the retired in particular and older people in general.

The present investigation of nonsupervisory personnel focused upon the same questions, although the questionnaire was altered to some extent to take account of the differences between the two groups of respondents. It was sent to about seventeen hundred individuals in the winter and spring of 1980. Responses were received from approximately eight hundred and fifty. We had anticipated that the response rate to the second questionnaire would be somewhat lower than the very high response for the first questionnaire. We found the overall response rate of about 50 percent to be gratifyingly high, considering that it was a mail questionnaire and taking into account that its recipients were nonsupervisory personnel, some of whom could have been expected to regard with some misgivings a questionnaire asking questions about retirement experience. It is also probable that the poor educational background of some of the recipients may have caused them sufficient difficulty in responding to the questionnaire that they decided not to respond.

Those individuals who did respond gave evidence of having answered the questionnaire carefully and in general thoroughly. Questions dealing with earnings and income are usually considered to be sensitive, so the somewhat lower response rate to these questions was not surprising. In addition to answering structured questions, the respondents were encouraged to provide us with comments about their experiences and about policies dealing with the retired and with older people in general. As in the case of the first survey, a very large proportion of respondents availed themselves of the opportunity to write about the details of their experiences and about their opinions and feelings. Their enthusiastic and often extensive comments encourage us to believe that the survey tapped a rich vein of concern on the part of most of the respondents.

To achieve the highest possible response rate, the recipients of the questionnaire were asked not to sign them and were assured that their anonymity would be preserved. At the time they sent in their completed questionnaire, they were asked to send in a postcard indicating that they had responded. Several weeks after the questionnaires were sent out, a second mailing was sent, asking the recipients to return their questionnaire or, if they had never received or no longer had the first one, to reply by postcard so that a second questionnaire could be sent to them.

CHAPTER 2
The Retirement Decision

Overview of Reasons for Retirement

The questionnaire asked the respondents to indicate why they retired. Only three of the 849 respondents gave no reason; most respondents gave more than one reason. Those who retired before reaching mandatory retirement age gave, on the average, two and a half reasons. Those who retired at mandatory retirement age were less apt to indicate a second or third reason, but even this group gave an average of one and a half reasons. Respondents were encouraged to give "other reasons" for retirement and to describe these in their own words. More than a quarter of the respondents who answered described such reasons in addition to those listed.

In order of decreasing frequency of response the reasons for retirement given by the 846 respondents were as follows: I could afford to retire, 34 percent; I had worked long enough, 33 percent; the pressures of work were getting too great, 24 percent; I had reached mandatory retirement age, 24 percent; my health made it necessary to retire, 18 percent; my health made it desirable to retire, 12 percent; I did not like the way older workers were being treated by management, 12 percent; my health qualified me for Social Security benefits, 10 percent; it did not pay to keep working, 10 percent; I did not like the way older workers were being treated by supervisors, 9 percent; my company offered me a special pension arrangement, 8 percent; my health qualified me for benefits from my company's benefit plan, 8 percent; my supervisors suggested that I retire, 6 percent; I did not like the way older workers were being treated by other employees, 3 percent; and I was laid off, 2 percent.

Several comments are in order. Although 24 percent of the respondents indicated that they retired because they had reached mandatory age, a cross-tabulation of reasons for retirement by age at retirement reveals that a small percentage (about 4%) of respondents who said that they retired because they had reached mandatory retirement age had not actually reached that age. With the elimination of this anomalous group, the percentage of respondents who retired because they had reached mandatory retirement age becomes 20 percent.*

Three in ten stated their health made it either necessary or desirable to retire, making health-related reasons for retirement the third most important category. If all respondents who indicated that they did not like the way older workers were being treated (by management, supervisors, or fellow employees—some respondents checked more than one), are grouped together, about one out of six respondents is included. Similarly, combining all respondents who gave the receipt of a disability benefit, either Social Security or company, or both, as a reason results in a group that constitutes 14 percent of the respondents.

We have formed another major category by combining those respondents who reported that they retired because of pressures of work and/or treatment of older workers by management, and/or supervisors, and/or fellow workers. This category includes about three out of ten of the respondents. The rationale for this grouping is that all the reasons are related to a facet of working conditions that was considered to be either unsatisfactory or burdensome by the respondents. Support for this assumption was provided by the fact that a considerable proportion of the respondents who indicated that the pressure of work was a reason for retirement also referred to (mis)treatment of older workers. In addition, many of the respondents provided written comments on the nature of the work pressures and treatment of older workers which they found undesirable.

*The lists of retirees who were sent questionnaires were drawn by each company so as to include 20 percent who were mandatorily retired, and this is a further indication that our respondents were fairly representative of the panel that received the questionnaire.

Using the regrouped categories of reasons for retirement, the following rank order for the 846 respondents and the percentage of respondents emerges: could afford to retire, 34 percent; had worked long enough, 33 percent; health-related reasons for retirement, 30 percent; pressures of work and treatment of older workers, 30 percent; mandatory retirement age, 20 percent; receipt of disability benefits, 14 percent; did not pay to keep working, 10 percent; special pension to retire, 8 percent; retirement suggested by supervisor, 6 percent; and was laid off, 2 percent.

As other studies of early retirement have found, we found health-related reasons to be either the most important or among the most important reasons for the decision to retire. When we confined our respondents to those who retired before reaching mandatory retirement age, the proportions who stated that they had retired for the four major reasons were slightly higher: almost two out of five say that they retired in part because they could afford to and/or had worked long enough; one-third report that health-related reasons and/or pressures of work contributed to the retirement decision.

The proportion of our respondents who indicated that their retirement was at least in part occasioned by health-related reasons varied sharply with age: two-thirds of those who retired at age 50–54 gave health as one of the reasons for retirement. Only three out of ten of the retirees who were 60–64 mentioned health. Respondents who were 65 were very unlikely to give health as a reason for retirement.

Although more than a third of the respondents who retired before mandatory retirement age indicated that health-related reasons were among the reasons for retirement, only one-sixth of them were qualified at retirement for disability benefits, either from Social Security or from their company benefit plans.

A cross-tabulation of major reasons for retirement by major reasons for retirement (Appendix D, 1) emphasizes the extent to which respondents gave more than one of the six major reasons. Respondents who reported that being able to afford to retire was a reason for retirement were also apt to say that they had retired because of a combination of pressures of work and treatment of older workers and also to indicate that they retired because they had felt that they had worked long enough.

Respondents who gave health as a reason for retirement were also likely to say that pressure of work along with treatment of older workers and qualification for disability benefits were associated reasons for retirement. They were less likely to say that they retired because they felt that they could afford to. Even so, one-quarter of those who gave health-related reasons for retirement indicated that they also felt that they could afford to retire. They were much less apt than were respondents who reported being able to afford to retire to say that they retired because they felt that they had worked long enough.

Respondents who gave pressure or treatment of older workers as a reason for retirement were also likely to say that their health contributed to their retirement decision and that they had worked long enough. It is probable that being subjected to excessive pressure or to treatment that was resented would induce workers to feel that they had worked long enough, but it is also possible that workers who had been on the job for many decades and who had little likelihood of further promotion or stimulating job change would begin to feel pressures of work or to believe that older workers were not being treated properly by their company.

In general, those respondents who gave mandatory retirement as reason for retirement were least likely to give other reasons. Even so, one out of five of them indicated that they had worked long enough. Although being retired mandatorily was clearly apt to be an overriding and sufficient reason for retirement, it is worth noting that only one out of ten of this group indicated that health status was another reason for retiring when he or she did. One out of fourteen of the mandatorily retired, however, indicated that he or she was able to qualify for disability benefits at the time of retirement.

Those who said that they had retired because they felt that they had worked long enough, among other reasons, were quite likely to say that they also retired because they could afford to; in addition they indicated, as we have noted above, that pressure of work and treatment of older workers contributed to their retirement decision.

In general there seem to be three underlying clusters of reasons for retirement. The first cluster is a respondent's feeling (a) able to afford to retire, (b) dislike of pressure of work or treatment of older workers, and (c) that he or she has worked long enough. Another cluster of related reasons for retirement center around (d) health-related reasons, (e) pressure of work or treatment of older workers, and (f) qualification for disability benefits. Finally, those respondents who retired because they had reached mandatory retirement age form a third group, even though a small proportion of them gave additional reasons for retirement, particularly that they could afford to (21%) and that they had worked long enough (19%).

The Timing of the Retirement Decision

Respondents were asked to say how long in advance they had known when they would retire and to indicate whether in retrospect they had retired at about the right time, too late, or too soon. A quarter knew when they would retire at least three years before they took that step, another quarter had between one and three years' foreknowledge. At the opposite extreme one in seven did not know in advance when he would retire, one in six had less than three months' foreknowledge, and a quarter had between three months' and a year's foreknowledge.

In discussing the relationship between foreknowledge of retirement and other aspects of the preretirement situation and postretirement experiences, we have grouped together those respondents who said that they knew the date of retirement less than three months in advance with those who reported that they did not know in advance. The respondents then fall into four equal-sized groups.

Respondents in the two youngest age groups, 50–54 and 55–59, were much less likely to have had much foreknowledge of the timing of their retirement. This is particularly true of the youngest age group. Four out of five of them report that their decision to retire came with foreknowledge on their part of three months or less. Almost two out of three of the age group 55–59 had no more than three months' foreknowledge. At the opposite extreme of age, three-quarters of those retirees who retired at age 65, the mandatory retirement age, said that they knew three years or more in advance when they would retire.

Another way of interpreting their response is that the great majority of those who actually did retire at mandatory retirement age had not even considered retiring earlier. Another group who indicated relatively longer foreknowledge of retirement retired at age 62, the year in which they became eligible for reduced Social Security benefits. Respondents in this group, however, were unlikely to say that they knew more than three years in advance when they would retire, only one out of eight claiming that degree of foreknowledge. A third of them said that they knew from one to three years in advance, and a third said that they had from three months to a year's foreknowledge. It seems apparent that the decision to retire at age 62 and accept reduced Social Security benefits was usually made with only a moderate lead time.

A far higher proportion of those respondents who reported that they had retired too soon said that they had little foreknowledge of retirement. Almost half said that they knew when they would retire only three months or less before the actual date of their retirement. It will be recalled that the younger age groups were more likely to have little foreknowledge. In almost all those aspects of their retirement experiences about which respondents expressed any degree of satisfaction, a relatively short period of foreknowledge was associated with a high degree of dissatisfaction or disappointment.

As far as the incidence of the various types of postretirement activity (including work experience) is concerned, there was no marked difference between those respondents who knew well in advance when they would retire and those who had relatively little foreknowledge of the date of their retirement.

In sum, foreknowledge of the date of retirement is related to relatively few aspects of the retirement decision and postretirement experiences. But in these limited areas, some clear conclusions can be drawn. A short period of foreknowledge is associated with (a) those who retired at relatively early ages, (b) those who gave health as a reason for retirement, (c) those who express dissatisfaction with their postretirement experiences, and (d) those who in retrospect are most likely to feel that they retired too soon.

It is to that issue that we now turn. Looking back at the timing of their retirement decision, what did the respondents feel at the time of the survey? Did they retire too soon, at about the right time, or too late? For the great majority of respondents, the answer is that on balance they believe that they retired at about the right time. Almost none of the respondents, only 2 percent, felt that they had retired too late. About one out of five said that his retirement decision came too soon. There was considerable difference between the respondents of the three companies in this respect, however. Only about one out of eight of the respondents who had worked for Utility felt that he had retired too soon, in contrast to the one out of four Chain Store respondents who said that his decision came too early.

The relationship between attitude toward the timing of retirement and age is interesting: almost three out of ten of the youngest age group felt in retrospect that they had retired too soon. It should be recalled that this same age group had much the largest proportion of respondents who said that health reasons made it either necessary or desirable to retire, almost two-thirds of them giving health as a reason for retirement and two out of five reporting eligibility for disability benefits. Since it is probable that many of the respondents in this age group who had serious health problems did not feel in retrospect that they had retired too soon, it is likely that an even higher proportion of the respondents who were aged

50 to 54 at the time of retirement, but who were in relatively good health, felt at the time of the survey that their decision to retire was made too soon.

On the other hand, the respondents who were 62 at the time of their retirement were overwhelmingly content with the timing of their retirement decision, only one out of ten reporting that it was too soon. In contrast, almost three out of ten of the respondents who were mandatorily retired at age 65 felt at the time of the survey that their retirement came too soon, another indication of the fact that a good proportion of the nonsupervisory workers who were retired mandatorily would have opted for continued work if it had been possible.

Retirement Expectations

We have already noted some striking differences between age groups of respondents with respect to the proportions who felt that they had retired too soon. But it is with respect to (a) expectations about retirement, (b) the extent to which these expectations were fulfilled, and (c) work experience during retirement that differences between respondents who felt that they had retired too soon and the other respondents are most clear-cut.

In general, both those respondents whose expectations of satisfaction during retirement were least rosy and those respondents whose expectations were disappointed, both in general and in respect to income and their social life, were much more apt to feel that they had retired too soon. In contrast, only one out of eight of the respondents who had expected retirement to be very pleasant felt that he had retired too soon.

Among the relatively small group of respondents who expected that retirement would be unpleasant, almost one-half reported that retrospectively they felt that they had retired too soon. Comparing their retirement expectations with their experiences, only one out of twelve of those who reported that their retirement experiences were more satisfactory than they had expected said that he had retired too soon, while again almost one-half of the respondents whose retirement experiences were less satisfactory than they had expected felt that they had retired too soon.

In particular, those respondents whose income was less than they had expected and whose social life was not as satisfactory as they had anticipated were likely to assert that their retirement had come too soon. Even more striking is the difference between those respondents who made large adjustments to cope with economic pressures and those who made little or no response. Almost a third of the former group felt that they had retired too soon; only one out of eight of the latter wished he had retired later.

Those respondents who felt they had retired too soon were much more likely than other respondents to have work experience during retirement. Thirty-five percent of them had some work experience, as opposed to 21 percent of those who were satisfied with the timing of their retirement. Even more striking is the fact that almost twice as large a proportion of the respondents who felt they had retired too soon were working at the time of the survey—22 percent—compared with 11 percent of the respondents who were satisfied with the timing of their retirement.

Moreover, the respondents who felt they had retired too soon were much more likely to say that they were working for economic reasons only, one-quarter of them reporting this, compared with 10 percent of those satisfied with their retirement timing. In contrast, three out of ten of the respondents who were satisfied with the timing of their retirement went to work in retirement for social reasons only, compared to about one-sixth of the respondents who felt that they had retired too soon.

Moreover, those who had retired too soon were much more likely to work full time and full year. The nature of the relation between the timing of retirement and postretirement activity seems to point in one direction. Respondents who felt that they had retired too soon were under greater economic pressure, took more active steps to meet this pressure, were less satisfied with retirement, were more likely to work, and when they did work were more likely to work longer schedules. It is clear that discontent with retirement timing was converted by a significant proportion of those who expressed it into positive action, particularly into work experience.

This seems to be true also with respect to their attitude to work in the future. Only slightly more than one-half of the respondents who were satisfied with their retirement timing indicated that they would consider work in the future. In contrast, almost three out of four of the respondents who felt that they had retired too soon would consider work in the future. The fact that those respondents who felt that they had retired too soon were much more likely to report some postretirement work experience and even present work experience* gives us some confidence that our constructed

---

*Two categories of postretirement work are utilized: (a) worked postretirement, including work at the time of the survey or sometime in the past 12 months, and (b) worked postretirement, but not during the past 12 months or at the time of the survey.

Table 2.1   Preretirement Plans, by Area (percentage
distribution of respondents)

Area of planning	Percentage distribution of respondents (N=849)[a]
Where to live	31
To move to a new location	16
How to spend their time	36
Planned to work	13
Planned to engage in home maintenance	32
Planned to engage in old hobbies	38
Planned to engage in new hobbies	24
Other planning	32

[a]Denominator equals all respondents.

measure of future work intentions has captured at least part of our respondents' intentions with respect to work in the future.

Planning for Retirement

Respondents were asked a number of questions about their preretirement planning and about the guidance, counseling, and information they had received in arriving at their retirement decision. The areas of preretirement planning and the percentage distribution of respondents are shown in Table 2.1.

It is evident that a large proportion of the respondents did not make plans with respect to a wide variety of possible activities. On the other hand most of the respondents did indicate that they had planned for at least one of the above activities or decisions. Noteworthy is the fact that only one out of eight of the respondents planned for some kind of work after retirement.

A number of planning areas were combined to provide a more concise basis for relating planning activities to preretirement circumstances and postretirement experiences. Respondents were separated into those who reported: (a) planning for retirement residential location (all respondents who said that they planned where they would live and/or to move); (b) planning how to use time (all respondents who said that they planned how to spend their time, to engage in home maintenance, and/or to engage in old or new hobbies); (c) planning to work during retirement; or (d) none of the above.

Respondents who retired because they felt they could afford to were least likely to plan for work and most likely to plan how to use their time and where to live. In contrast, those respondents who retired because of pressure or treatment and/or mandatory retirement requirements were more than twice as likely to plan to work as were respondents who said that they could afford to retire, that their poor health contributed to retirement, or that they had worked long enough.

The relationship between planning to work and actual work experience is of particular interest. Four out of five respondents who said that they had planned to work reported that they did indeed work during retirement. The consistency between planning for work and carrying out these plans is striking, taking into consideration that some respondents reported that they were unable to secure employment, either because there were no job opportunities or because of age discrimination or unsuccessful job searches. Some of the respondents who had planned to work also undoubtedly encountered unforeseen health problems, either on their own part or on the part of their spouses, that prevented gainful employment.

On the other hand, it is also evident that a considerable proportion of the respondents who actually did work at some time during retirement had not planned to do so. Of those respondents who reported that they had worked only a relatively short part of their retirement, almost three-quarters had not planned to work at all. Of those who reported that they had worked most months, almost one-half had not planned to work. Finally, of those who said that they had worked almost every month during retirement, two out of five had not planned to work.

In other words, while planning to work during retirement was usually translated into actual work experience, most of those who actually did work during retirement had not planned to work. Only two out of five of the approximately two hundred respondents who reported some work experience during retirement had actually planned to work.

Those respondents who said that they had planned to work during their retirement were much more likely than other respondents to indicate that they would have responded to company policy designed to alter the timing of the retirement decision. Only one out of six of these respondents indicated that he would not have responded to a set of suggested company policy initiatives. For almost seven out of ten, such policies might have induced later retirement, and two out of five said that company policies designed to induce earlier retirement might have had that effect upon them. For the respondents as a whole, only one-third indicated that appropriate company policies might have induced them to delay retirement, while another one-fourth said that they might have been induced to retire earlier. About a third said that none of the suggested company policies with respect to older workers would have changed the timing of their retirement.

In general, those respondents who planned one or more aspect of their retirement experience seem to have felt that planning was useful. Almost one-half said that their planning was very useful, and another one-third reported that planning was of some use. About one-fifth, however, said that planning was either not very useful or of no use at all. The fact that such a large proportion of respondents did indicate that planning was very useful indicates that this is an area where further efforts to improve the preretirement planning process could be expected to lead to more satisfactory retirement experiences.

Planning for retirement and the retirement decision itself are related to the kinds of information and counseling that are available to individuals who are involved in making decisions about retirement timing and subsequent activities. Only one-half of the respondents indicated that they received significant amounts of counseling from their companies before they retired. One out of six said that a good deal of counseling was received, another three out of ten said that they received some counseling, but more than a third said that they had had no counseling. Two out of five were satisfied with the amount of counseling they received, but a quarter reported that they believed that more counseling would have been desirable. In contrast, about a quarter said that they thought that counseling was neither necessary nor desirable.

In the light of the fact that a majority of the respondents received little or no counseling, the fact that a quarter of the respondents felt that more counseling would be helpful is sufficient reason for companies to make an effort to improve both the depth and breadth of their counseling efforts. Obviously, the role that company-provided counseling can play in improving the quality of retirement decisions and the character of postretirement life is inherently limited. This is in large part because the information that is used by the potential retiree to make his decision about retirement and his planning for postretirement activities comes from a very wide range of sources, of which the company from which he retired is only one and not always the most important.

Nevertheless, the respondents indicated that their company was on balance a relatively important source of information. But it should also be noted that more than a quarter of the respondents indicated that they did not receive any useful information or guidance about retirement. Since networks of friends and relatives are usually one of the most important, if not the most important, source of information and guidance about critical life decisions, particularly with respect to labor market information and guidance, it is somewhat surprising that our respondents were twice as likely to give their former company as a source of information and guidance than they were their friends and relatives. Again, this would seem to indicate that companies, although already playing a significant role in this area, might well put greater efforts into giving information and developing guidance techniques that would be useful to older workers and to those who are contemplating retirement. We have already seen that a considerable proportion of our respondents knew when they would retire at least a year, and often at least three years, in advance of the actual date of their retirement. In this period of foreknowledge of retirement, planning, guidance, and counseling efforts would be most effective.

Expectations at Retirement

Respondents provided us with information about how satisfactory they expected their retirement experience to be before they retired, as well as their anticipations as to the rate of inflation.

Respondents who retired from Utility or Chain Store were slightly more likely to look forward to a very satisfactory retirement. One out of ten of the Manufacturer respondents reported that he or she expected retirement to be to some extent unpleasant, whereas only about one in twenty of the other two companies expected retirement to be unsatisfactory.

There was little difference among the respondents with respect to expectations about retirement in general except for those respondents who retired in 1978, the last year covered by the survey. Whereas about two-thirds of the respondents as a whole looked forward to a very pleasant retirement when they retired, respondents who retired in 1978 were less sanguine. Only slightly more than one-half of them felt that retirement would be very pleasant. This sudden and sharp decrease in the proportions of respondents who expected a very pleasant retirement may be linked to increased anxiety about continued and rapid inflation.

Respondents who retired when they were in the youngest age group, 50–54, or in the oldest age group, 65, were least likely to expect a very pleasant retirement experience. Less than half of the first group expected a very pleasant experience and less than three out of five of respondents aged 65. The fact that such a high proportion of the younger age group also reported health problems is probably a major part of the explanation of their relatively pessimistic expectations, while many of the respondents aged 65 at retirement seemed to resent the fact that they were forced to retire. For those respondents for whom work itself was either a pleasant experience or for whom their job or the working environment provided important personal satisfactions or support, mandatory retirement might well have led to anticipations that retirement would not be very pleasant.

High-skill white-collar workers seem to have had higher expectations about retirement than did blue-collar workers generally, particularly low-skill blue-collar workers, only three-fifths of whom looked forward to a very pleasant retirement. Those respondents who knew well in advance when they would retire also had more rosy expectations about retirement than did those who had only slight or no foreknowledge. Of the latter group, those who had three months or less foreknowledge, only about one-half looked forward to a very pleasant retirement. But again, it should be kept in mind that a sudden and severe health problem which forced early retirement was one reason for respondents not knowing well in advance when they would retire. It is understandable that where retirement was synchronous with severe and sudden health problems, expectations would not be optimistic.

A cross-tabulation of retirement expectations with actual retirement experiences (Appendix D) reveals that, in general, retirement experiences were at least as satisfactory as the respondents had anticipated, or even more satisfactory. This is particularly the case with those respondents who said that they had expected their retirement to be very pleasant. One-half of them reported that retirement experiences were about what they had expected, and a third reported that they were even more satisfactory. Only about one out of ten was disappointed. For those who anticipated an unpleasant retirement experience, about three out of ten were more satisfied than they had expected to be, but one out of five felt that the actual retirement experience had turned out even worse than expected.

That expectations tended to be realistic is also indicated by the relationship between preretirement expectations and responses to economic pressures. Almost one-half of the respondents who had believed that their retirement experience would be unpleasant reported that they had had to make large adjustments in their life

style to cope with economic pressures. In contrast, only one out of
ten of the respondents who had looked forward to a very pleasant
retirement reported that he too had had to make large adjustments. When a comparison is made of the retirement expectations
in general with detailed aspects of retirement life, it is evident that
those who had expected a relatively unpleasant retirement were
much more likely to report that their income was less than they had
expected it to be (two-thirds of them so reported) and that their
social life was worse (again, two-thirds felt this). Those respondents
who looked forward to a very pleasant retirement reported that
their income was more than expected as often as they reported that
it was less, and they were overwhelmingly likely to report that their
social life was better than they had expected it to be (three out of
four reported this).

The experience of respondents with respect to health was also
generally favorable. Respondents who expected retirement to be
very pleasant and those who expected it to be unpleasant were
likely to feel that their health was better than they expected it to be
(three out of four of the first group and two out of three of the
second). It is somewhat surprising that respondents were in general likely to report that their health was better than they had expected it to be (seven out of ten of the respondents felt this). Considering the fact that the mean number years of retirement for our
respondents was six and a half years and that their mean age at the
time of the survey was about 67, it would seem that not only the
passage of time but also the fact that on the average they were well
past 65 at the time of the survey would have caused a number of
respondents to have had unpleasant shocks with respect to health.
A possible explanation for the fact that the great majority of the
respondents reported better health than they had expected is that
those individuals who were sent questionnaires but who did not respond were the ones most likely to have experienced health problems.

Respondents who had not anticipated a pleasant retirement experience were somewhat more likely to have worked during their
retirement, but these were also the respondents who tended to feel
that their income during retirement was lower than they had expected it to be. They were also more likely to have made large adjustments in their life style in response to economic pressures. As
one might expect, those respondents who had not expected a pleasant retirement and who worked during their retirement years were
also more likely to say that they worked for economic reasons than
were respondents who expected a very pleasant retirement (see Table 2.2).

Table 2.2 Employment During Retirement by Retirement Expectations (percentage of respondents)

Expectations	Employment			
	About every month	Most months	Not many months	None
Very pleasant	7	4	12	78
Somewhat pleasant	7	8	10	75
Unpleasant	11	2	15	73

Not only did the respondents who expected an unpleasant retirement tend to have a higher rate of postretirement work experience, they were also much more likely to work full time. Again, it is likely that their expressed dissatisfaction with their economic circumstances was translated into positive actions, such as paid employment.

Expectation of an unpleasant retirement was also closely related to marital status. More than seven out of ten of the respondents who looked forward to a very pleasant retirement were married at the time of the survey, while only about one-half of those who expected an unpleasant retirement were married.*

We have already had occasion to mention in several contexts the expectations of respondents about inflation. Only about one in twelve of the respondents reported that expectations of the rate of inflation during retirement was more or less in line with what occurred. Slightly more than a quarter, while not having realistic expectations, still anticipated that there would be moderate inflation. Four out of ten did not expect much inflation at all. About one-quarter of the respondents indicated that they had not given it much or any thought, and if they did think about it at all, they had not thought it would be very rapid.

Few differences are evident among the respondents of the three companies. A somewhat higher proportion of Utility respondents anticipated at least some inflation, and respondents from this com-

*Seventy-six percent of the respondents were married at retirement. This had declined to 69 percent by the time of the survey. It is unlikely that the decline in the percentage of respondents who were married altered to any significant extent the proportions given in the text, although they were a few percentage points higher at the time of retirement.

pany were less likely not to have given inflation much or any thought. A point of some interest is whether recent retirees were more realistic in their estimation of the rate of inflation than were retirees who retired in the early part of the period, 1968–1978.

If the retrospective opinions of the respondents about the degree of inflation that would occur are accepted as a reflection of their actual opinions at the time of their retirement, their responses seem to indicate that there was little change in anticipations about the rate of inflation over the period. A distinct difference is evident, however, between the two end years, 1968–1969 and 1978–1979. Although a considerable proportion of both groups had very unrealistic anticipations (or did not give it much thought), the more-recent retirees were more likely to anticipate at least some inflation and conversely less likely to give the matter little or no thought. Even so, while almost three out of ten of the respondents who retired in 1968–1969 recollected that they gave the matter little or no thought, the same was true of one out of the six of those retired in 1978.

Even discounting to a considerable degree the extent to which the respondents, particularly those who retired in the early part of the period, were able to recall accurately their anticipations of inflation, it still seems likely that a very large proportion of the respondents, whatever the year of their retirement, had quite erroneous beliefs about the extent to which they would be faced with rapid and continuous inflation.* That such erroneous anticipations included such a large proportion of the most-recent retirees is somewhat surprising.

Perhaps there is a deep-seated reluctance on the part of people, particularly when they are 60 or older, to accept such a fundamental change in their conception of the way the economy functions as is implied by continued and moderately rapid inflation. There must have been a pervasive confidence on the part of many of our respondents, regardless of the year of their retirement, that in spite of a succession of years marked by inflation before their retirement, somehow the powers-that-be would be able to bring inflation under control in the immediate future. On the other hand, there is some indication that this confidence was beginning to erode in the last part of the period covered by this study.

Examination of postretirement work experience in the light of anticipations of inflation reveals that a far smaller proportion—

---

*It seems plausible that many of the respondents who retired in the early part of the period credited themselves with more foresight than they actually possessed at the time of retirement.

only one out of ten—of those respondents who had realistic anticipations of inflation (those who reported that they anticipated that
inflation would be as fast as or faster than what actually occurred)
had any work experience in retirement. In contrast, about a quarter of the respondents who reported that they anticipated that
prices would increase nowhere near as rapidly as they have increased, or that they gave inflation little or no thought, had some
work experience during retirement. On the other hand, there is little evidence, except for the group of respondents who believed that
prices would rise even faster than they did, that realistic inflationary expectations might have been associated with a decision to delay retirement.

CHAPTER 3

Postretirement Work Experience

The Decision to Work After Retirement

About one-quarter of our respondents—about 200 persons—told us that they had some work experience during the years of their formal retirement from their companies. The intensity of work experience varied widely. One in fourteen said that they had been employed almost every month, and another 5 percent indicated that they had worked "most months." One out of eight therefore had work experience either almost all months or "most months" of their retirement. On the other hand, about one in ten of the respondents indicated that his or her work experience was of limited duration.

In addition to being asked whether they had had any work experience during retirement, respondents were asked whether they were employed at the time of the survey or during the 12 months preceding the survey. One-eighth of the respondents indicated that they were employed at the time of the survey, and another 4 percent had had work experience during the 12 months preceding the survey. In other words, one-sixth of our respondents—about 140—indicated either that their work experience had occurred during the previous year or that they were presently working. In the discussion that follows, the term "currently employed" refers to both those who were working at the time of the

Table 3.1   Reasons Given for Postretirement Work (N=200)

	Percentage of respondents who worked postretirement
Only economic reasons (income, inflation)	15
Only social reasons (contact with people, like work)	28
Both economic and social reasons	47
Neither economic nor social reasons (idiosyncratic)	10
Total	100

survey and those who had worked at any time in the 12 months preceding the survey.

The proportion of respondents who had some form of work experience during retirement varied to a considerable extent between the three companies. Chain Store respondents were much more likely to have had work experience: about one-third worked some time during their retirement and almost a fourth were currently employed. At the opposite extreme were the Utility respondents. Only one out of six had had any work experience during retirement, and only one out of ten was currently employed.

Those respondents who had had any work experience during retirement were asked why they had chosen to work. Among the approximately 200 respondents who had worked at all, slightly more than one-half (55%) indicated that one of their reasons was a desire for more income. One-third of the respondents gave inflation as a reason. The most frequently cited reason given for choosing to work after retirement, however, was that the respondent "liked working," two-thirds of the respondents giving this as one of their reasons. In addition, two out of five of the respondents who had work experience stated that they chose to work at least in part because they wanted more contact with people.

Two of the reasons given, desire for more income and inflation, are clearly of an economic character. Choosing to work because of a desire for contact with people or simply because the respondent liked to work are, in our view, social reasons for working. Since respondents could give more than one reason for working and generally did, we have grouped their responses in Table 3.1.

Almost one-half the respondents said that both economic and social reasons were involved in their decisions to work after retirement. It is interesting to note, however, that among the respondents giving either exclusively economic reasons or exclusively social reasons for working, social reasons were almost twice as common as economic reasons. Almost three out of ten of the respondents with work experience worked exclusively for social reasons. Only about one out of six respondents said the only reason for working after retirement was economic. Another way of looking at these responses to questions about the reasons for postretirement work experience is provided by the following summary:

	Percentage of respondents who worked postretirement
Social reasons, either exclusively or in conjunction with economic reasons	75
Economic reasons, either exclusively or in conjunction with social reasons	62

Work experience after retirement is associated more frequently with strongly held social values (the importance of work or its intrinsic satisfactions and the value of social relationships available in a working context) than it is with economic pressures. But is is also clear that the majority of the respondents who made a decision to work after retirement felt the stimulus of both economic and social motives.

Before they retired many of those who worked after retirement planned to work. Of the approximately 100 respondents who planned to work after retirement, only one-fifth said that they had not worked during retirement. On the other hand, of those who had some work experience during retirement, only about two out of five had planned to work.

Even among the group of respondents whose health problems were severe enough to entitle them to private or public disability benefits, one in ten worked at some time during retirement. At the opposite extreme, of those respondents who said that pressures of work and/or the treatment of older workers were among the reasons for taking early retirement, more than three out of ten had some type of work experience after their retirement. Perhaps even more revealing is the fact that slightly more than one-quarter of those who were mandatorily retired had subsequent work experience, in spite of the fact that their age at retirement was 65 or nearly 65 (about one out of five of the retirees who was mandatorily retired was younger than 65, reflecting the retirement policy of one of the companies up to the early 1970s).

The Nature of Postretirement Work Experiences

THE JOB SEARCH

Those respondents who worked for an employer during retirement were asked about their job search experiences. An overwhelming proportion indicated that their job search had been very short. Six percent did not search at all but responded instead to a job offer. Of those who did search, more than half said that they secured employment immediately, and another quarter said that their search was successful within a month. One out of ten said that the search took from one to six months, and one out of fifteen said that the search lasted longer than six months. A small proportion (5 percent of those with work experience) indicated that they had given up the search, usually after no more than six months of searching, and worked as self-employed individuals.

Respondents who had some work experience were also asked how they obtained employment after their formal retirement. Many of the respondents gave more than one method, since many had held more than one job. More than half the respondents indicated that they had obtained jobs through family, friends, or other personal contacts. About one-quarter had obtained their jobs by applying directly to the employer. Only one out of five indicated that either employment agencies (private and/or public) or want ads were the means by which he or she obtained employment. About 5 percent indicated that they had obtained a job through the company from which they retired.

It should be kept in mind that we are limiting the discussion at this stage to those respondents who worked at all during their retirement. In a later section we will look at those respondents who wanted work but, for one reason or another, did not obtain it. In sum, it is evident that those respondents who did work for the most part obtained employment quickly, usually through a network of relatives, friends, and acquaintances or through their own direct

applications to possible employers. For a small proportion, however, a relatively short job search had a discouraging effect that led
to self-employment as an alternative.

THE TYPE OF EMPLOYER

Respondents who had postretirement work experience were asked
to indicate what types of employers they had worked for. Slightly
less than two-thirds of the respondents with work experience
worked for companies, another fifth worked for private individuals, and another fifth were self-employed. The character and size
of these companies contrast sharply with the companies from
which the respondents had retired. Almost half of these companies
employed less than 50 individuals. Slightly more than one-quarter
employed more than 250 people and even in this category, more
than half employed less than 1,000 people. Only one out of ten of
the respondents who worked during retirement worked for a company that employed at least 1,000 people.

The contrast between the size of the companies for which our
respondents worked after retirement and the size of the companies
from which they had retired is extraordinary. Since most of our respondents indicate that they obtained jobs relatively easily, it seems
probable that a large proportion of them actually preferred to
work for a small employer or at least did not make a strong effort
to obtain employment from a large company. It should be kept in
mind, however, that the company from which our respondents had
retired may possibly have been the only very large employer in the
communities in which they lived (and the size of the unit within
which the respondents actually worked before retirement may often have been quite small, because the three companies had plants
or installations in a very large number of communities).

The respondents were also given an opportunity to tell us what
kind of company employed them. Here again there is a difference
between the type of company our respondents typically worked for
before retirement and the type of company they worked for during
their retirement years. Only about one in ten of the respondents
indicated that his employer was a utility. On the other hand, almost
half the respondents indicated that their postretirement employer
was engaged in retail trade. Almost two out of five said that they
were employed by companies that were neither manufacturing,
utility, nor retail establishments.

Finally, the respondents reported striking differences between
the type of work experience they had before and after retirement.

Two out of three said that their postretirement job was very different from their preretirement job. Only one out of six said that the
work he performed after retirement was similar to what he did before retirement.

The fact that both their postretirement jobs and employers
tended to differ considerably from their preretirement counterparts did not seem to have a negative effect on most of the respondents' satisfaction with their postretirement work experience.
Indeed, respondents tended to be at least as satisfied with their
postretirement work experience as they were with their preretirement work, one-third reporting more satisfaction and only one-
fifth, less.

It is also interesting to note that those respondents who stated
that they had worked almost all the time during their retirement
(about a third of all respondents with postretirement work experience) were much more apt to say that their job during retirement
was different (72%) and that their satisfaction was greater (42%).

We have already noted that almost all the respondents had
worked for several decades or more (in many cases for all of their
worklife) for the companies from which they retired. Similarly,
most of the respondents who had work experience during retirement worked for only one employer. Almost two-thirds of them
had only one job during retirement. Another fifth had two jobs,
while one-sixth had three or more employers. It will be recalled
that a considerable proportion of the respondents who had worked
during retirement worked either almost all months or most months
of their retirement years, and it is therefore evident that many of
the respondents who had work experience worked for only one
employer for a considerable period of time.

This fact is the more noteworthy since most of the respondents
who were employed by a company worked for small firms, a large
proportion of which (44%) were retail establishments. Moreover,
many of them, as we shall see, did not work full time or full years.
Even so, it is clear that the great majority of them stayed with either
one employer or were employed by two employers, at the most.
Apparently not only do early retirees who go back to work during
their retirement prefer stable employment relationships, but such
relationships seem readily available to the kind of early retirees
who were typical of our three companies, workers who had very
stable employment records with the company from which they retired.

This is the case in spite of the fact that most of the respondents
who worked during their retirement worked at jobs that were dif-

ferent from those they had held previously, in the majority of cases very different. Apparently it is not the kind of skill or experience that the respondents offered to their postretirement employers that was the critical factor in their being able to enter stable employment relationships, but rather the personal characteristics they brought as stable and reliable employees.

Respondents who had work experience during retirement tended to work part time and part year. A quarter of the respondents usually worked close to a full week, while another quarter worked less than 20 hours a week. Only a third reported that they usually worked at least 48 weeks a year, while three out of ten usually worked less than 20 weeks a year.

A comparison of the usual workweek and work year, which includes all respondents with work experience during retirement, with the workweek and work year of respondents who were working at the time of the survey reveals that respondents presently working tended, as we would expect, to put in many more weeks per year and more hours per week than those respondents who had some work experience during retirement but who were not working at the time of the survey.

A fifth of the respondents who were employed at the time of the survey were working full-time, full-year schedules or very close to such a schedule. Another fifth of the respondents presently working were working full year, but with somewhat reduced workweeks (20 to 35 hours). About a quarter of them were working moderate work years (20 to 48 weeks) and moderate workweeks (20 to 35 hours). Another group, about a sixth, worked moderate work years (20 to 48 weeks) and relatively short workweeks (less than 20 hours). Only a very small proportion (one in twenty) worked both short workweeks and short work years (less than 20 hours and less than 20 weeks).

Looked at in another way, the cross-tabulation of hours against weeks worked reveals that 70 percent of the respondents who were employed at the time of the survey had work schedules of at least 20 hours a week and 20 weeks a year. This fact confirms the impression produced by other evidence, qualitative as well as quantitative, that a large proportion of the respondents who worked during retirement had strong commitments to stable and relatively extensive amounts of work. But these respondents represented only a subgroup of the respondents who had worked at some time during their retirement. Those respondents who, even though they had worked sometime during retirement, were not working at the time of the survey displayed a pattern of shorter workweeks and work years than did those who were presently working.

As well as being asked how many weeks per year and how many hours per week they worked, respondents were asked to indicate their preferred work schedules. In general, preferences closely matched actual work schedules. It seems clear that there is enough flexibility in most local labor markets to offer most early retirees who wish to work after their formal retirement a choice of job opportunities that permit them to work about as many hours a week and as many weeks a year as they desire. But a note of caution should be added. Since respondents were offered only three possible lengths of workweek and work year and the intervals were necessarily quite large, it is possible that some respondents may have felt that their actual work schedule did not exactly meet their desires or needs.

In addition, it is evident that in a few instances respondents who might have worked, if they had been able to locate jobs with the desired work schedules, were prevented or inhibited from working by an inability to locate employers who could match their needs either for shortened workweeks and work years or for flexible working schedules. This point will be analyzed in greater detail later.

Finally, although many of our respondents emphasized in their comments the importance of noneconomic motives for work during their retirement years (a fact confirmed by their responses to the structured part of the questionnaire dealing with reasons for postretirement work), most of the respondents also indicated that one of the reasons for working was their need or desire for additional income or a concern about the impact of inflation upon their standard of living. How well did the respondents do in earning additional income?

Since such questions are often perceived to be an invasion of privacy and to result in a significantly lower response rate, respondents were not asked about their earnings during the entire year prior to the survey. We did, however, ask our respondents to indicate both the hourly wage and the fringe benefits they usually received in their postretirement work and to compare it to what they received before retirement.

The answer to the question "How well did our respondents do in earning additional income?" is that in terms of hourly earnings and fringe benefits, they did quite poorly, on the average. It seems certain that they were not often lured back into employment after their formal retirement by wage offers above what they had been earning when they retired!

A cross-tabulation of hourly pay by whether the respondent was presently employed or had been employed during the 12 months preceding the survey provides us with the clearest evidence about

Table 3.2   Hourly Wage Rates of the "Currently Employed"
            (percentage distribution)

Hourly wage rates	Employed at time of survey	Employed during the 12 months preceding the survey
Less than $3.00	10	8
$3.00-3.99	39	50
$4.00-4.99	18	12
$5.00-6.99	14	23
$7.00-9.99	12	4
$10.00 or more	7	4
Total	100	100

hourly wage rates at the time of the survey (winter–spring 1980, see Table 3.2).

More than 50 percent of the respondents who had work experience during the 12 months up to the survey (most of whom were working at the time of the survey) were earning less than $4.00 an hour! These were individuals who had worked on average about 25 years for the same company before they retired. In February 1980 the gross average hourly earnings, nationwide, of production or nonsupervisory workers was $6.45. The average hourly pay of the respondents who reported hourly earnings during the 12 months preceding the survey or at the time of the survey was $5.32. A small group of respondents who were working at the time of the survey received commissions rather than a wage and therefore did not report an hourly wage.

But it is the comparison of their hourly wage with their preretirement hourly earnings that shows the most shocking disparity. The following comparison of postretirement with preretirement rates includes all respondents who were employed by an employer during their retirement years, rather than just those respondents who were presently working or had worked during the previous 12 months. The data show that a drastic cut in hourly pay occurred for the vast majority of respondents who had postretirement work experience. Of the respondents who worked postretirement, 48 percent earned less than half their preretirement rates; 13 percent, about half their preretirement rates; 17 percent, more than half but less than preretirement hourly earnings; 9 percent, about the same; 9 percent, somewhat more; and 3 percent, a lot more. This pattern provides strong corroboration of the assertion of a large number of respondents who claimed they did not work after retirement because it did not pay to work (153 of the respondents gave this as a reason for not working).

Even worse than the situation with respect to hourly wages was the pattern of postretirement fringe benefits. Respondents were asked to compare fringe benefits in their postretirement jobs with those received before retirement. In their postretirement jobs, 71 percent received no fringe benefits; 16 percent received much less fringe benefits than in their preretirement jobs; 5 percent, somewhat less; 6 percent, about the same; and 3 percent, more than in their preretirement jobs.

When it is remembered that the respondents had retired from three companies which were among the most generous nationally with respect to fringe benefits, it is clear that the total rewards from work, hourly earnings plus fringe benefits, were drastically lowered for most of the respondents who reported postretirement employment and earnings. Although our respondents were limited to nonsupervisory workers, many of them were highly skilled workers with extensive vocational education and long years of experience with companies whose average pay scales compared very favorably with the economy as a whole.

When hourly wage rates of respondents who reported that they had worked during retirement for economic reasons are compared with those who said that they worked for social reasons (liking for work or desire for social contacts) a somewhat unexpected result emerges.

It appears that those early retirees who have work experience during their retirement years primarily for social reasons tend to reject very low-paying jobs but are contented with jobs that have very modest hourly wage rates. A higher proportion of those respondents who worked during retirement for primarily economic reasons were able to secure relatively better-paying jobs, although some were willing to accept very low wage rates. The explanation may be that some of the respondents reporting that they worked for economic reasons were hard pressed to find any job, while others of this same group were strongly motivated to seek out as high-paying jobs as they could find. Those respondents who worked for social reasons may have been more willing to accept jobs that offered considerable social and work satisfactions, even though the hourly rate of pay was more moderate.

In order to cast additional light upon postretirement decisions

about work, we asked the respondents a series of questions relating, first, to their attitude toward possible or actual postretirement work experience on their own part and, second, to work
activity by older workers or the retired, in general.

Among those respondents who reported working at all after retirement, only one in five resented having to work during retirement in order to have enough to live on. This is the same proportion of those who reported that their postretirement work
experience offered less satisfaction than their preretirement work.
An even smaller group (about 12%) resented that their skills and
experience had not been recognized by their postretirement employers.

On the other hand, a much higher proportion of the respondents who had worked postretirement reported two types of satisfactions. More than two-thirds of them were happy to discover that
their skills and experience were appreciated. One-half said that
they were happy to work because it enabled them to do things at
work which they could not do before they retired.

Some of the changes from preretirement to postretirement jobs
were: assembler to a self-employed bicycle repairman; transformer
name-plate stamper to a salesman of sporting goods; maintenance
engineer to caretaker; market researcher to income tax preparer;
salesman to security guard; division head (together with family) to
owner and manager of lodge and cottages in a resort area; design
draftsman to installer of burglar alarms; installer and repairman to
clerk in a sports and taxidermy shop; equipment technician to engineer on steam tourist railroad; service technician to church dea-
con; expeditor to carpet installer; sales person to business manager
for a symphony society; and shipping and stockroom worker to cat-
tle farmer.

Positive attitudes toward postretirement work were expressed by
many of the respondents. Two-thirds of them believe that a retiree
should be able to work if he or she so desires. And only one out of
six believes that older workers should make room for younger
workers. On the other hand, two out of five of the respondents said
that if "a retired person has planned properly for retirement and
what he can do after retiring, he usually will not want to work."

The Decision Not to Work

In spite of severe inflation and changed legal and social attitudes
toward work by older persons, a decision *not* to work was made by
three out of four of our respondents—about 640 persons.

In the analysis of the decision not to work, the respondents are divided into two groups—the 640 respondents who had not worked at all during their retirement, and the much smaller group of 55 who had worked at some time, but not during the previous 12 months. In the case of the second group the focus will be upon why they decided to stop working. Also of interest is whether either the first or the second group might, at some time in the future, consider working. Do they represent a pool of potential workers? Would changes in policies which affect older workers either before or during retirement, and the continuation of the present inflation, or both, lead them to reconsider the desirability or the continued viability of complete retirement?

There is a clearcut relationship between the extent of post-retirement work and the different reasons given for retirement (since respondents could, and often did, give more than one reason, the actual relationships are complex). The least likely of the retirees to work after retirement were those who said that they were receiving disability benefits either from Social Security or from their company benefit plan. But even in the case of these individuals whose health limitations have been confirmed medically, one out of ten indicated that he or she had postretirement work experience.

Another group (which undoubtedly includes a large proportion of those receiving disability benefits but also includes a number of individuals who said that their health made it desirable, rather than necessary, to retire), whose likelihood of postretirement work experience was relatively low, were those who gave health-related reasons for retirement. About a quarter of the mandatorily retired, a relatively older group, reported postretirement work, as did a fifth of those who retired because they felt that they had worked long enough. Working long enough, for some of these individuals, apparently meant long enough for the company from which they retired (but recall that about a half of the respondents had worked thirty years or more for one company—time enough for many to feel that they had worked long enough). For others, economic pressure was a spur to resumption of work after retirement.

The groups most likely to work after retirement were (a) those who retired because of pressures of work or treatment of older workers and (b) those who gave idiosyncratic reasons for retirement (e.g., they wanted to move closer to grandchildren, they were tired of a long drive to work and wanted to work nearer their residence, etc.).

Those respondents who did not work during their retirement years were asked why. Among the major reasons are the following:

there are no job opportunities, 9 percent; health does not permit work, 29 percent; does not pay to work, 27 percent; do not want to work, 53 percent; have encountered age discrimination, 4 percent; unsuccessful job search, 2 percent; and other reasons, 13 percent.

Among the respondents who did not work, much the most important reason for their not working is that they did not want to work. But it should be noted that several respondents who gave this reason also indicated in their comments that this reason was becoming less compelling. Some mentioned that they were getting restless, some that they were afraid of inflation, others that a change in their own health or that of their spouse might make work more attractive or necessary in the future.

Next in importance to an aversion to continued work is the inhibiting effect of health limitations. It is interesting to compare the respondents who said that their health situation contributed to their decision not to work during retirement with those who gave it as a reason for retirement. Of the 250 who gave health as a reason for retirement, only about one-half also gave health as a reason for not working after retirement. One hundred and fifty-five of the respondents reported that their health situation made it necessary for them to retire, and another 102 said that their health situation made it desirable for them to retire. Only 155 of the respondents, including some who did not retire because of health, said that their health situation was among the reasons for not working during retirement. In other words, almost 260 respondents said that they retired because their health situation made it either necessary or desirable for them to retire, but a much smaller number said that health was a reason for not working after retirement. It may, of course, be that the health situation of some respondents, possibly a fairly large number, changed for the better. It seems more plausible, however, that the number of respondents with serious health problems would increase with the passage of time. Moreover, since the respondents retired between 1968 and 1978, a considerable proportion were much older at the time of the survey than when they retired.

Perhaps more significant is the fact that more than a quarter of the respondents said that a reason for not working was that it did not pay, a view confirmed by the relatively low hourly wage rates of the respondents who were working. The perception that hourly wage rates would in all likelihood be much lower than what they had received in their last years of employment, coupled with a belief that they might lose a considerable proportion of their Social

Security benefits, undoubtedly contributed to the idea that it "simply didn't pay."

Because of the significance of the decision to work or not to work during retirement, the relationship between postretirement employment (or its absence) and the reasons given by respondents for retirement was explored.

Of the group of respondents with no work experience during retirement, 35 percent gave as a reason for retirement that they could afford it, while another third gave health-related reasons. A sizable number also retired at least in part because of pressures of work and treatment of older workers. It is possible that a significant portion of these particular nonworkers during retirement would consider returning to work under satisfactory conditions.

There were three principal reasons given for not working during retirement: (a) health, (b) "It does not pay," and (c) "Do not want to work." As expected, most of those who gave health as a reason for not working also indicated that health was a reason for retirement. Not all of them did so, however. Apparently the health status of some respondents changed so that, although they had not retired for reasons of health, their health deteriorated during retirement to the extent that it became a reason for not working during retirement. On the other hand, we have already noted that a relatively small proportion (17 percent) of those who gave health as a reason for retirement did engage in work during retirement. Nonetheless, only a few of these, about 6 percent of the respondents who gave health as a reason for retirement, worked relatively continuously during retirement.

Almost half of those who reported that they did not work in retirement because it did not pay reported that they had retired because they could afford to. Half of those who did not work during retirement because they did not want to also said that they had retired because they could afford to. But this relationship can be read another way. *Only* half of those who reported that they did not work in retirement either because it did not pay or because they did not want to had retired in part because they could afford to. One out of three respondents who did not work during retirement (because (a) it did not pay or (b) they did not want to work) had retired in part because of pressures of work or treatment of older workers. It would seem therefore that many of these respondents might, if the economic pressures upon them increased or if work itself became more attractive, either economically or socially, return to work at some time in the future, even if only to a limited degree.

To Work or Not to Work: Those Were the Questions

A small group of slightly less than 60 respondents who had worked at some time during their retirement, except during the year before the survey, deserves special attention. They represented about one in three of the respondents who had worked at all postretirement but who had stopped working, at least for a year, when the survey was carried out. We addressed several questions to them in order to determine, first, why, after having decided to go to work after retirement, they then decided to cease working. Second, we were interested in whether this group of individuals might go back to work at some time in the future and, if so, under what circumstances.

Almost all the respondents (57) who had worked during retirement but not in the 12 months before the survey gave one or more reasons for no longer working, most of them only one. About a third reported that they had stopped working because of a health problem (35%). A quarter said they no longer wanted to work (26%). A sixth (16%) indicated that they could not find a suitable job, and another sixth (17%) said that it did not pay to work. A quarter of these respondents (26%) reported that other reasons were involved in their decision to stop working. These included health problems of spouses, transportation problems, desire to travel for an extended period of time, and so forth.

Several of the answers of this same group of respondents to questions designed to elicit whether or not they might return to work, and under what conditions, are closely related to the reasons they gave for ceasing to work, with one important exception.

More of these respondents (31%) indicated that they would resume work if a suitable job were available than had indicated that they had stopped working because they could not find a suitable job. It is probable that some of those who said that they had stopped working because it did not pay failed to report that lack of a suitable job was a reason for ceasing to work. Some of these may have reported that they would go back to work if a suitable job became available, meaning by that a job which did in fact "pay."

It seems plausible to conclude that many of those who said that they had stopped working because of their health would return to work if their health situation improved, and so reported 29 percent. Some of the respondents (14%) indicated that a removal of the earnings limitation imposed by Social Security would result in their reentering the labor market. Much the most frequently given reason for possibly resuming work, which was given by half the respondents who had some work experience during retirement but who had not worked in the 12 months preceding the survey, was continued inflation.

If it is correct to assume that most of the respondents who indicated that health reasons prevented their continuing to work did not report that continued inflation would induce them to resume work, then a very high proportion of the respondents who had stopped working for one or more of the reasons other than health might be induced to at least attempt to reenter the labor market. Also it seems likely that present attitudes about what constitutes a suitable job, as well as about whether continued work pays or not, might be significantly altered by long-continued inflation. It may also be that this group represents something of a bellwether, since they seem to have some of the characteristics of a swing group. They resent the limitations on earnings connected with Social Security benefits, they are quite anxious about continued inflation, and some of them report that they are not working because no suitable jobs are available. A change in any of these factors could alter, perhaps significantly, the number of individuals who work during their retirement years.

The Possibility of Future Work by Respondents Who Had No Postretirement Work Experience

Those respondents who did not report any work experience during retirement were not asked directly whether they intended to work at some time in the future. Instead, all respondents were asked what kind of work schedules they would prefer if they were to return to work. Slightly more than one-half of the 642 respondents who reported no work experience during retirement responded to questions dealing with work schedules in the future. Although it cannot be concluded that a positive response to these questions is equivalent to an intention to work sometime in the future, a willingness to state distinct preferences for hours worked per week and weeks worked per year is at least an indication that, under certain circumstances, those respondents who did give answers might consider working in the future.

Two-thirds of the respondents who reported that they had not worked during retirement because no suitable job was available responded to the questions about future work schedules. It seems probable that many of the respondents who did not work in retirement because they felt there were no suitable jobs would in fact work if their requirements for work schedules, type of employment, and hourly pay, coupled with fringe benefits, were approximately met.

Nevertheless, an examination of actual hourly pay rates and fringe benefits secured by respondents who were at work at the time of the survey does cast serious doubt on the possibility that respondents whose definition of a suitable job included pay schedules approximating what they had been earning at retirement will, in fact, find such jobs. Moreover, the work schedules in the future that respondents who had no work experience during retirement indicated that they would prefer were distinctly shorter than the work schedules of those respondents with postretirement work experience. It may therefore prove difficult, especially in relatively small or constrained labor markets such as those confronted by many of the respondents, to provide a sufficient number of jobs for respondents who have quite firm preferences for short and flexible working schedules.

Almost three out of five of the respondents who reported health limitations as a reason for not working during retirement did not respond to the work schedule questions. The fact that two out of five did, however, may indicate that a number of respondents would in fact consider work if their health situation improved. Since respondents with health limitations form the largest group of respondents without work experience during retirement, with the exception of those who do not want to work, substantial improvement in their health status or in working conditions, which would make it easier for them to work in spite of health problems, might induce a considerable number of them to reenter the labor market.

If a positive response to the questions about work schedules in the future can be taken as implying at least a possible consideration of work in the future, it is challenging that almost one-half of those who said that they did not work in retirement because they did not want to still answered the work schedule questions. They may represent a group that is finding itself increasingly under economic pressure and increasingly anxious about further inflation. They may also include a number of respondents who reported that they had retired because they no longer wanted to work, particularly because of problems with inflexible work schedules and long journeys to work, but now were becoming increasingly restless and at loose ends. It is plausible that a decision to retire because one has worked long enough is not necessarily irreversible. Several years of retire-

ment may be enough to induce a significant number of early retirees to reconsider whether or not and under what conditions they
might prefer working. Anything which either increases the net return for postretirement work or increases the economic pressure
felt by this group of respondents would be apt to induce at least
some of them to return to work. Any quite large change in either
circumstance might induce many to reconsider their nonwork status during retirement.

Finally, almost all the respondents in two small groups of respondents who did not work in retirement, (a) those who reported
an unsuccessful job search and (b) those who said that age discrimination was a reason for not working, indicated some preference for
a future work schedule. Indeed, the fact that nine out of ten of
these respondents, whose desire to work in retirement was probably quite positive, also answered the work schedule questions gives
us additional ground for believing that the questions about future
work schedules did tap to some extent the desires and intentions of
many of the respondents who had no work experience but would,
even if only under specific and quite limiting circumstances, consider work in the future.

Feelings About Work

A good proportion of the retirees in this study felt at the time of
retirement that they had worked long enough and could afford to
retire. Although many subsequently reevaluated the timing of their
retirement and came to believe that they might have retired too
soon, a substantial number were relieved to get away from their
job. The feeling was prevalent that younger workers were paid
more favorably for the same work, got promotions more easily, and
did not work as hard. Many retirees felt tossed aside and neglected.
One complained, "Young people were getting to me. Ask them to
do something, they'd tell you do it yourself." Another complaint
was having to take orders from workers who were younger and less
experienced, which made some of the older workers feel inferior.
Others complained that hiring and training programs favored minorities or the young. A poor relationship with one's boss or supervisor was another reason for deciding that the work environment
was too pressured and the relief felt at retiring. One worker told of
having had a heart attack at her desk, not being allowed to go
home, and being threatened with the loss of her job if she didn't
come to work the next day.

Joan S. had been an executive secretary for 23 years before

retiring in 1972 at the age of 58. She felt that older workers were treated poorly by management and that she was forced by her boss to retire with no advance planning. "I feel my age caused the personality clash that made my retirement come about earlier than I had planned," she writes. "I would have been better off being fired—so I could at least claim unemployment compensation—instead of being placed in the predicament I found myself in."

On the other hand, many who were not working became restless and viewed working for pay as a form of therapy—a means of staying healthy and alert, as well as a way of demonstrating one's worth. Quoting his mother-in-law, one retiree wrote, "All men should retire until 65, then go to work because they aren't worth a damn at anything else."

Returning to work after retirement became a problem for some who didn't want to take jobs of less status, pay and/or responsibility than they had had before retirement. Others reported difficulties in being judged overqualifed when they did look for lower-level employment. A substantial number attributed both these problems to age discrimination. In the words of one retiree, "Though the mind is still sharp, when you mention your age, a noticeable coolness comes between yourself and a possible employer." Another retiree suggested the need for a government program similar to CETA to help retirees get part-time work to supplement their income, or more corporate involvement in the creation of part-time jobs for older workers. Having retirees work a few hours for public services in exchange for credits toward utilities and property taxes was another suggestion.

CHAPTER 4
Unpaid Activities

Two major groups of questions in our questionnaire were designed to obtain information about nonwork activities. In one set of questions, retirees were asked to estimate the number of hours per week they usually spent engaged in volunteer work, hobbies and recreation, routine domestic chores, and home maintenance and improvement.* In another set of questions, retirees were asked specifically about the nature of their hobbies and recreation, and about shifts in frequency of activities from before retirement to the previous 12 months.

Volunteer Work

The amount of time spent in volunteer work was related only loosely to the amount of time spent working for pay. In general, retirees who were not involved with one were not involved with the other. Retirees who were moderately involved in volunteer work (1–10 hours in a typical week), however, tended also to not have worked for pay in the past year. Only 6 percent of our retirees

*The percentages based upon hours reported spent in various activities in a typical week are approximate percentages based upon assumptions we made that nonresponses in part of the activities section of the questionnaire meant zero hours if other parts of the activities section were completed.

spent more than ten hours per week in volunteer activities. Of these persons, most were not working at all for pay. Volunteer work might be a substitute for paid work in this group. Those doing any volunteer work at all and those heavily involved in it said more frequently that they would consider paid work in the future than those not doing any volunteer work at all.

Differences emerged in the social characteristics of those who adopted different patterns of volunteer work. Women were more likely to do volunteer work than were men and were also more likely to spend more hours per week at it. Fifty-five percent of men did no volunteer work at all in a typical week, compared to 45 percent of women. In addition, the majority of those spending more than ten hours per week in volunteer activities were women. The better educated were also more likely to do volunteer work and to spend more hours at it than were those who had not completed high school.

Age and the length of retirement were also related to volunteer work patterns. We compared those who had retired in the first five years of the ten-year span of retirement years included in the study to those who had retired in the six most recent years. Those who had been retired longest were more likely than more-recent retirees to be heavily involved in volunteer work. This involvement, however, may depend upon health as one becomes older. Retirees involved with volunteer work were more likely to report that their health was better than they expected it to be and that they believed that they were at least as healthy, if not healthier, than other retirees their age. Those who retired at the youngest ages (50–59) were less likely to spend time in volunteer work than those who retired at later ages. This was not, as pointed out earlier, because they were using the hours not spent in volunteer work to earn income. For these youngest retirees, particularly those who were 50–54 years of age when they retired, failing health was an issue and placed limitations upon activity.

Volunteer work patterns also varied by company. Manufacturing retirees were least active in volunteer work. Seventy-one percent did no volunteer work at all in a typical week, compared to about three-fifths of those in the other two companies. Those who had worked more than thirty years for the same company were also more likely to do volunteer work and to spend more time at it than were retirees who had spent shorter amounts of time with their preretirement companies.

There were several other differences between those not involved in volunteer work and those involved to a moderate and to a high degree. Those more involved in volunteer work were more likely to feel that they had retired later than they ought to have retired and that their retirement was more satisfactory than they had expected. They were also more likely to report having more family income and a better social life than they had expected.

Laura H. is an example of a retiree who presently devotes large amounts of her time to volunteer work—more than twenty hours in a typical week. Since she would rather work as a volunteer than in a paid job, she volunteers the secretarial services for which she used to be paid as an employee at Chain Store. She considers her volunteering to be appreciated and respected and believes that having some regular activity has prevented her from retiring to a "rocking chair existence." After working for Chain Store for 38 years and retiring ten years ago at the age of 63, her current annual income is between $10,000 and $15,000—enough money, in her opinion, so she can retire from paid work and make gifts to her local church. Having never married, she finds that her volunteer work gives her more contact with people than she would otherwise have.

Jim C. also devotes more than twenty hours in a typical week to volunteer work for his church. An insurance agent, he retired in 1972 at the age of 59 after 22 years with Chain Store. He felt that his health, combined with the pressure of his job, made it desirable to retire. Impossible assignments from his supervisor led him to feel he had worked long enough. Surprisingly, his health subsequently was better than anticipated, but his income has been less. This has also caused him to take a paid, part-time job for the past ten months as a security officer for a lumber company. Before that he did not work for pay. Mr. C.'s total family income is presently between $10,000 and $15,000, and he finds it necessary to dip into his savings a bit and sell some of his stock to get by. Aside from his part-time work, his activities are centered on religious affairs: helping to build a new church, singing in the choir, and working as financial secretary and Sunday school teacher are some of these activities. "Working for the Lord can be very satisfying," he reports.

Hobbies and Recreation

There was a relationship between time spent in volunteer work and time devoted to hobbies and recreation. Those who had neither hobbies nor recreational interests tended to do no volunteer work. There were, however, a significant number who did no volunteer work but were highly involved in their hobbies and recreation. Those who were highly active in volunteer work were generally highly active in hobbies and recreational activities as well.

In all three companies, the majority of retirees spent at least an hour per typical week at their hobbies and recreational interests. About a third spent more than ten hours per week, and about a quarter reported spending no time at hobbies and/or recreation. Manufacturer retirees were least likely to involve themselves with hobbies and recreation after retirement.

Hobbies and recreation and paid work are no substitutes for one another. Those who spent no time engaged in hobbies and recreational interests also generally did not work for pay. Perhaps, as in volunteer work, this low activity pattern is a manifestation of health difficulties. Retirees with low activity patterns in hobbies and recreation did tend to perceive their health as worse than that of others their age and worse than they had expected. On the other hand, of those who were not currently working for pay, most spent either moderate or a large number of hours (more than ten per typical week) with their hobbies or recreational interests. Among those working for pay, it was typical to spend a moderate number of hours engaged in hobbies and recreation. Those with large time allocations to hobbies and recreation were less likely to have worked for pay in the previous year.

The amount of time spent with hobbies and recreation was also related to the amount of time spent working, if a retiree was working for pay. Those who spent between one and ten hours per week with their hobbies and recreation were more likely to spend less than ten hours per week working for pay.

Unlike activities patterns in volunteer work, women were slightly less likely to spend time with hobbies and recreational interests, but contributed more hours to these activities when they were involved with them. Both the better educated and those with family incomes above $20,000 in the previous year allocated more time to hobbies and recreation.

A high degree of involvement in hobbies and recreational activities was also related to the year in which a person retired. Similar to the case with volun-teer work, those who had been retired longest (who had retired between 1968 and 1972) were more likely than more recent retirees to either spend no time with hobbies and recreation or, the opposite extreme, to be highly involved with hobbies and recreational interests. As pointed out above, like those completely disengaged from volunteer work, involvement with hobbies and recreational interests may depend upon health as one becomes older.

Table 4.1 Time Spent in Hobbies and Recreational Activities
Before Retirement and in Last 12 Months

	Never			Often		
	(1)	(2)		(3)	(4)	
		Last 12	Change (2 minus		Last 12	Change (4 minus
	Before	months	1)	Before	months	3)
Active sports	38	46	8	20	20	0
Gardening	20	18	-2	40	48	8
Travel	6	11	5	24	30	6
Attend sports events, movies, etc.	20	29	9	13	13	0
Watch TV, play card games	3	1	-2	48	60	12
Hobbies	17	12	-5	28	47	19
Adult education	61	66	5	6	7	1

High involvement with hobbies and recreation was also related to satisfaction with retirement and the perception that one's social life was better than had been expected.

Table 4.1 shows shifts in specific activity patterns in hobbies and recreation retirement in the previous twelve months. The activities engaged in most frequently in the previous twelve months were hobbies, gardening, watching TV, and playing card games. These were also the areas in which there were greatest shifts after retiring. The activity engaged in with least frequency was taking adult education courses: only 7 percent of our retirees had taken courses often in the previous 12 months. Surprisingly, active sports were also engaged in rather frequently by 20 percent of our retirees.

Whether or not a retiree was currently working for pay affected choices of nonwork activities in the past 12 months. Those who were working were also more likely to be involved often in active sports, the attending of sports events, movies, etc., and travel and adult education while they were working. Those who were not working became more frequently involved in watching television and playing cards, as were those who earned less than $4 an hour in their postretirement work. Those who worked the greatest number of hours per week were least likely to be engaged in some of the favored activities of more moderate workers—active sports and gardening. These appeared to be the activities most expendable if one had to choose between spending more time at paid work and spending more time with hobbies and recreational activities. The relationship of a retiree's involvement with paid work to his time allocation to travel was more complex. Often, a retiree had to work at least a minimum of hours per week to enable him or her to afford traveling. If a retiree worked too much, however, it could mean too little free time to travel.

Those whose health had been better than they had expected it to be in retirement were generally more likely to be frequently involved in activities than were those whose health had been worse than they had expected. Those who felt their health was worse than other retirees their age tended to shift to activities such as watching TV, playing cards, or taking courses in adult education, which would presumably require less expenditure of physical energy.

Social characteristics of retirees were related to involvement in different activities. Those with the most education (more than 12 years) were more likely to involve themselves often in active sports, the attending of sports events, movies, travel, and adult education in retirement. In contrast, retirees who did not complete high school were more likely to involve themselves often with watching TV and playing card games. Patterns within the previous year resembled preretirement patterns. Retirees who had been involved in a specific activity before their retirement tended to continue it afterward as well. Similarly, activities that had held little interest for retirees before retirement continued to hold little interest for them after retirement.

Those with more income than they had anticipated also tended to involve themselves to a greater extent with activities in retirement different from those who had less income than they had expected to have. Gardening and travel were engaged in more frequently by those who perceived themselves as being better off economically than they had expected. On the other hand, those who perceived themselves as being worse off economically than they had expected tended to be engaged more often in watching

TV and playing card games. In general, those with the highest total family income tended to be more frequently active in all hobby and recreational categories except watching TV and playing cards.

Differences were also apparent between those who retired between 1968 and 1972 and those who retired more recently. The latter were more active in most activity areas, but, surprisingly, active sports and travel were not among the activities which slackened off as retirement lengthened. In fact, recent retirees travel slightly less. It may be that retirees in the 1968–1972 retirement group will slow down more as they get older. There seems to be a lessening activity pattern in particular among those who retired in 1968 or 1969 compared to those who retired in the early 1970s.

Social characteristics related to recreational patterns included gender. Men are more likely than women to participate frequently in active sports. High involvement in most other activities is generally a female pattern, however. Women more frequently travel, watch TV, play cards, and attend sporting events, movies, etc. Those who were recreationally active generally had a spouse who had also stopped working at the time of their retirement who, we suspect, shared many of their recreational interests.

Company differences also existed. Chain Store retirees were the most active in almost all recreational areas.

Greater satisfaction with one's retirement was not necessarily a by-product of a highly active recreational pattern. Yet, the type of activity in which the retiree involved himself or herself did, in some cases, make a difference. Those highly involved with the relatively passive pursuits of watching television and playing cards found retirement less satisfactory than they had expected. They also judged their social life in retirement to be worse than they had expected, in contrast to retirees who, in general, were frequently involved in recreational activities, and who were more likely to say that their social lives in retirement were better than they had expected. A further indication of the importance for retirement of the specific type of recreational activity with which a retiree becomes involved is the relationship between type of activity and attitude toward the timing of retirement. Retirees who were highly active in the more physically demanding recreational activities (active sports, gardening, and travel) and those who were highly involved with their hobbies were more likely to think they retired too late, whereas retirees who were highly involved in the more physically passive recreational activities (attending sports events, movies, etc., watching TV, and playing cards) were more likely to feel that they retired too soon.

Active participation in sports is not necessarily related to other highly active recreational events, such as travel. Similarly, a passive activity, such as watching TV or playing cards, is not related to a configuration of relatively passive physical activities. Rather, retirees often appear to involve themselves in a combination of several levels of activity.

Joe L. is an example of a retiree highly involved with his hobbies after retirement. He was an appliance repairman for 27 years before retiring ten years ago at the age of 61. He retired because he could afford to, and although he considers inflation and the rising cost of living to be a serious problem for him, he has not gone back to work. His income is presently less than $10,000 a year, and he gets by through dipping into his savings. His hobbies are fishing, hunting, and gardening; he also does repair work for close friends and neighbors whom he does not charge for his services. He writes that he had many repair work opportunities for pay after retirement, but never sought paid work.

Like Mr. L., Bertha B. retired when she could afford to at the age of 61, after working as an office clerk for 25 years. She reports that she "wanted to be able to travel and have some fun before getting too old." She has not worked for pay since retirement, since she just doesn't want to work anymore. Instead she devotes more than twenty hours per week to hobbies and recreation and more than twenty hours per week to routine domestic chores. Widowed, she lives with her daughter and son-in-law. They both work and she keeps house for them. Her current income is less than $10,000, but since she lives with her children, she is able to travel and purchase tickets to shows. Her late husband's pension check helps, and she takes advantage of senior citizen discounts.

Routine Domestic Chores and Home Maintenance

The amount of time devoted to hobbies and recreation was closely related to the amount of time spent doing routine domestic chores, and was related to a somewhat lesser extent to the amount of time spent in maintaining one's home. Generally, about 43 percent of our retirees spent between one and ten hours in a typical week at routine domestic chores, and one-fifth claimed they spent no time at all in that activity. Thirteen percent were involved in maintaining their home to the degree of more than ten hours in a typical week, and about two-fifths of retirees claimed they spent no time at all in home maintenance.

Those who spend more time involved in routine domestic chores are more likely to have worked for pay in the past year but to spend fewer hours working for pay than those who allocate fewer hours per week to domestic chores. In contrast, those who devote more time to home maintenance are also more likely to have worked in the past year for pay, but to be working a greater number of hours.

Immersion in domestic chores may be a way of substituting for unsatisfying paid work. If working for pay, those whose time allocation to routine domestic chores is heavy tend to find their present work less satisfying than their preretirement jobs. Those who spend more time in routine domestic chores also tend to be female, somewhat less educated, and to be earning a lower hourly wage, which might also be related to a greater allegiance to a division of labor within the household based upon traditional sex roles and therefore a greater involvement with domestic chores, and/or a lesser likelihood of obtaining satisfying work. Those who are married, however, spend less time per week in routine domestic chores, possibly because the duties are more likely to be shared, although this may be more characteristic of our male retirees than female retirees.

There are fewer variables related to amount of time allocated to home maintenance. Generally, those more highly involved in maintaining their home tend to be male, married, with an income during retirement which is less than they had expected, coupled with a more recent retirement. Manufacturing retirees generally spend more time per week in home maintenance but less time per week in domestic chores, compared to retirees from the other two companies. Both those who are highly involved with routine domestic chores and with home maintenance perceive their health as better than other retirees their age. Yet, those heavily involved in domestic chores are also somewhat more likely to characterize their health as worse than they had anticipated, a puzzling contradiction.

Hours spent in paid work, volunteer work, hobbies and recreation, routine domestic chores, and home maintenance in a typical week were totaled in order to give an idea of the total activity pattern. Retirees were divided into three levels of activity: low activity (0–25 hours), moderate activity (26–49 hours) and high activity (50 or more hours spent at these activities). About two-fifths of the retirees in our sample could be considered low-active, and about two-fifths could be considered moderately active. About a fifth had a high activity pattern relative to the others. Activity pattern varied by company. Chain Store retirees were the most active, and Manufacturing retirees were the least active. Those who were generally

more active were more recently retired and more satisfied with
their retirement than they had expected to be. They also tended to
be better educated and in better health than others their age. Retirees who were highly active reported a better social life and better
health than they had expected during retirement, but not necessarily more income.

A varimax rotated factor analysis of the time-spent variables,
however, indicated that the unpaid activities, although related to
each other in number of hours per typical week, were independent
of time spent working for pay.

Overall, then, we can see a relationship between many of the
other variables in our study and time distribution patterns in the
areas of volunteer work, hobbies and recreation, routine domestic
chores, and household maintenance. Not only is degree of activity
related to other variables, but to types of unpaid activities, as well.
Time allocation patterns in one realm, as well as social characteristics, can affect activity patterns in other realms. Activity patterns
may then have subsequent effects upon feelings about one's adjustment to the retirement status. From the above examination of our
data, it is also clear that paid work and unpaid activity patterns are
very much connected within the life experience of particular retirees.

CHAPTER 5

Life After Retirement: Successes, Disappointments, and Reactions

From the general review of the fit between retirement expectations and postretirement experiences provided in Chapter 2, it is clear that most respondents, at least two in three, anticipated that retirement would be "very pleasant" and that there were few surprises for most people. More men than women claimed that the retirement experience was about what they expected, while more women than men found it even more satisfactory than anticipated. The largest number who found it less satisfactory were Chain Store retirees of both sexes.

Satisfactions centered around the feeling of having enough free time—to spend with family members, particularly grandchildren, or to spend doing things that they had always wanted to do. No longer having a boss and no longer needing to cope with the pressure and tension that accompanied their work were frequently mentioned as making retirement, in the words of one retiree, "the best job I ever had." Some simply said that there were no "worst things about retirement," that retirement was "like having a baby—wonderful if you have prepared for it."

Bill H., for example, worked for 27 years before retiring in 1976 at the age of 55. He retired when he felt that he could afford to and believes that he retired at exactly the right time. Having planned his retirement for years, this respondent thinks that planning is very important and has helped to make his retirement the wonderful experience that it is. Although he does not work for pay and does not wish to, he usually contributes between one and five hours per week to volunteer work. Most of his time, however, is spent on home maintenance and household chores. He also has been able to devote more time to fishing and gardening than he was able to before retirement. His family income is presently less than $10,000, although it was between $15,000 and $20,000 when he retired. One of the best things about retirement, he writes, is "the opportunity for my wife and I to spend our lives together." He also appreciates being freed from daily pressures and having the time to commune with nature. All told, he says, he is "pleased with the 27 years spent with _____ and thought they were fair in most ways. In fact, they made it possible for me to retire after only 27 years."

Respondents were also given the opportunity to indicate the full range of problems they had encountered in retirement and to check those they considered to be among the three most serious. The responses, grouped by the sex and company affiliations of the respondents, are summarized in Table 5.1. The overriding importance of three problems—inflation, the respondent's own health, and the health of the spouse—is obvious. These were indicated to be the three most serious problems associated with retirement. Many of the other problems listed may be accepted as indicators of the difficulties of social adjustment after retirement. The reactions to these groups of problems—inflation and income inadequacy, health, whether of self or of spouse, and the whole rubric of what can be classified as social problems—will be considered in turn.

Income and Inflation

The most frequently given reason for taking early retirement was that the respondent could afford to retire. While there was a distinct positive relationship between the percentage of respondents in each preretirement hourly wage class who gave this reason and the size of the wage rate, ranging from 24 percent of those earning less than $5 per hour to 67 percent of those earning $15 and more (the last class had relatively few members), the relationship does exhibit some anomalies. In the mid-range, $7.50 to $14.99 per hour, no more than 40 percent gave this reason; on the other hand, at least one in four, who, as has been indicated, earned the lowest wage rate, also gave this reason. To what degree were these expec-

Table 5.1 Problems Encountered Postretirement (responses as percentage of respondents)

	Male			Female		
	Util.	Mfg.	Chain Store	Util.	Mfg.	Chain Store
Inflation	91[a]	94[a]	93[a]	83[a]	91[a]	90[a]
Transportation	22	24	19	20	21	22
My health	41[a]	45[a]	40[a]	32[a]	42[a]	32[a]
Spouse's health[b]	41[a]	49[a]	30[a]	46[a]	62[a]	51[a]
Housing appropriate for retirement	6	8	7	14	9	10
Not enough friends or social life	7	18	9	14	17	11
Not enough to to do with my time	7	15	18	7	11	14
Too much time spent on home maintenance	21	24	11	20	19	16
Personal safety	22	16	17	22	19	19
Too little contact with relatives	12	11	9	12	11	13
Feel useless because not working	12	17	14	10	11	19

[a]Among three most serious.
[b]Base restricted to respondents with spouse.

tations about the adequacy of income in retirement validated by experience?

More than half of the Utility women reported that their economic situation was better than they had expected it to be. From 50 to 60 percent of the others found that their expectations had been too optimistic. Chain Store women voiced this complaint in above-average numbers, with more than 70 percent stating that their income was less than expected.

A small number, from 7 to 10 percent, more men than women, had either correctly anticipated the virulence of inflation in the previous year or had believed it would be even worse. About half of the men and two in five of the women, however, had seriously underestimated the course of inflation. In fact, about 20 percent of all the respondents and an even larger number of Manufacturer respondents reported they had not given much thought to the matter at the time they retired. (Year of retirement ranged from 1968 to 1978, a period with widely differing inflationary experiences.)

Expectations about the future course of the standard of living were on the whole gloomy; about seven in ten expected it to fall either somewhat or a great deal. About one in five of the respondents believed it would fall little or not at all, and a small number—about 10 percent—were optimistic that it might actually rise. Manufacturer women expressed the most pessimism of any group, and Manufacturer men echoed this sentiment to a greater degree than the men in the other two companies. As one former clerk put it, "I can't do many things I could do while working—miss my many friends, have little money for food and none for travel." A particular resentment was the smaller size of private pensions when compared to the pensions of government workers. Executives within their own company were also viewed as getting greater benefits upon retirement, at the expense of other workers.

A more severe aspect of the financial difficulties faced by some of these retirees was not having enough money to pay for basic food and health care needs, coupled with a reluctance to rely upon government programs. "Most of my generation is starving," wrote one retiree, "and too proud for welfare or medicaid. Our greatest fear is health care, especially extended nursing that might be necessary. The average individual does not have such resources." In the words of another retiree who felt that her pension was relatively low ($262 per month), considering that she had worked for a large corporation for 31 years, "Each day grows worse. I never thought this could happen. It's one big mess."

If the retiree's response during the 12 months preceding the survey to the economic pressures of inflation and receiving less income than expected took the form of selling his house, moving to cheaper housing, the sale of his car, or dipping into savings "quite a lot," it was considered "large." If the response took the form of "dipping into savings somewhat" or "sold some of my stock," it was classed as "moderate"; if none of the above, as "small."

About one-half of all the respondents reported having had to make only a small response to economic pressures, about one-third a moderate response, and only one in six, overall, a "large" response. Utility women seem to have been the best insulated from economic pressures, Manufacturer women the least. One in four of these women reported taking a type of action characterized as a "large" response. Manufacturer men were the most seriously affected of their own sex, with one in five reporting a "large" response; they were only marginally better off than the Manufacturer women.

Of course, returning to work is one predictable reaction for those who report serious economic pressure, and there is in fact a striking relationship between the size of total monthly benefits (defined as the sum of monthly Social Security benefits and monthly company pension received in the year before the survey) and postretirement work experience. There is an unmistakable tendency for the work experience of respondents during retirement to decrease as total monthly benefits increase.

Although respondents with work experience tended to report that they worked during retirement more for social reasons than for economic reasons, the data reveal that almost none of those respondents whose monthly benefits were in the highest two brackets had worked more or less continuously during his retirement. In contrast, almost one out of five of the respondents whose total monthly benefits were less than $400 had more-or-less continuous work experience.

In spite of the fact that the lower the total monthly benefits the greater the likelihood that the respondents had worked during retirement, those in the lower benefit classes were not much more likely than those in the upper to report that they worked during retirement for economic reasons only. And they were just about as likely to report that they had worked during retirement solely for social reasons and that social reasons for postretirement work took precedence over economic reasons. It is of course true that about half the respondents, regardless of their income level or the

amount of their total monthly benefits, indicated that both economic and social reasons entered into their decision to work during
retirement. Individuals who are under severe economic pressures
to work can be convinced at the same time that they are working
because they like to work or because they enjoy the social relationships available in the context of work. These same individuals, if no
economic pressure were impelling them, might well choose not to
work at all. That, at least, is what their responses, taken in combination with the expressed reasons for postretirement work given by
the respondents, seem to imply. It is appropriate to add that this in
no way diminishes the importance or the significance of social reasons for working during retirement.

Ray J. worked on an assembly line for thirty years until he retired
in 1972 at the mandatory retirement age of 65. Since retirement,
he has encountered many problems, the most serious being the rising cost of living, the declining health of his wife, and worry about
his personal safety. In the past year, he has had to cut his standard
of living and make substantial withdrawals from his savings for basic living expenses. Mr. J. has not worked for pay since retirement
and resents that he cannot find a suitable job. His present family
income is less than $10,000, including a pension of $222 a month
and Social Security benefits of $396 a month. "Retirement is very
good if you can afford it," he writes, "but when you get to seventy
years old, who wants to give you a job, and you don't feel right anyway." He adds, "The company gives you a small pension and it was
fair, but the way things are today, it's way out of line. I have a sickly
wife and cannot afford to pay for oil bills, but the federal government can give dollars to different countries, besides the billions of
dollars it spends on ammunition which no one can eat."

Jane S. worked for _____ for 32 years and retired in
1978 at the age of 62. She retired because she felt that the pressures of work were becoming too great, considering her health,
and that younger employees were being given advancement opportunities at the expense of older workers. Because of her health, she
qualified for special benefits from her company's benefit plan, and
at the suggestion of her supervisors she retired. Now, however, she
regrets having retired early. She did not expect her retirement to
be very pleasant, but it has been even more unpleasant than expected. Not prepared for the rate at which prices were rising, she
has had to move to cheaper housing and withdraw a large proportion of her savings. She would go back to work if she could find a
suitable part-time job, but at 64 years of age, she feels there are no
suitable jobs for people her age. She looked for a year and then

gave up, because it seemed useless to spend any more time looking for work. She wrote:

I only receive $77.77 a month. How about that for a 32 year employee? I cannot cash the stock because it is so low and I only get $345 every three months with Social Security. I can barely live—only the young employees will receive anything worthwhile. Not the old employees that helped to build the company.

Social Security was also often thought to be inequitable, particularly with regard to earning limitations and women. Many respondents said that benefits should go to the elderly, who have paid into the fund, and should not be used for other programs, such as disability. There was also a substantial amount of fear about the possible taxing of social security benefits, and fear was also expressed that benefits would be cut or that the Social Security system will ultimately collapse.

Health

In the area of health, most respondents were pleasantly surprised. About two in three found their health after retirement better than they had expected. This was particularly true of the men who, it should be remembered, gave health as the major reason for retirement. Manufacturer women, the smallest subset in the sample, fared the worst with 37 percent of them in worse health than they had anticipated.

Further, more than eight out of ten felt their health was better than or at least as good as that of other retired people their own age. Almost half the Chain Store men and women checked "better," as did more than one in three of the Utility women. On the other hand, more than one in six Manufacturer men felt themselves to be in worse condition than their peers, as did one in seven Utility men and one in nine Manufacturer women. This perception shared by so many that "own health" was better than expected may seem at variance with the priority given by so many to health as a reason for retirement and to "own health" as a postretirement problem. It is possible, however, that respondents may have had a serious health problem before retirement and simply found that it had not worsened with time.

Spouse's health as a problem in retirement was mentioned more frequently than own health by all respondents, with the exception of Chain Store men. For Manufacturer women and Chain Store women, spouse's health condition was significantly more worrisome than their own.*

Perceptions as to the status of one's health do not seem to be a significant predictor of postretirement nonwork activities. A comparison of time spent in four major postretirement nonwork activities, by those who gave "health" as a reason for retirement, with time spent by all other respondents in these activities reveals little difference between the two groups of respondents.

There is, however, some relationship between "health" given as a reason for retirement and postretirement work experience. The rate of postretirement work experience of those who gave health-related reasons for retirement is lower than that of the other respondents, although the difference is not as great as might have been expected, especially for those respondents who gave health-related reasons but not the receipt of disability benefits as a reason. Even in the case of the respondents who did give this reason for retirement, more than one in ten reported postretirement work experience.

On the other hand, those respondents who reported that their health was better than they had expected it to be were more apt to have had work experience. Slightly more than one quarter of them worked at some time during retirement, and one out of twelve had worked almost continuously since retirement. Those respondents who reported that their health was worse than expected were much less likely to have worked almost continuously since retirement, only one in about thirty reporting working to this extent, while only two out of ten reported any work experience at all.

It is clear that the effect of worse health than had been expected often took the form of a decrease in the continuity of work experience during retirement and of a decrease in the likelihood of being at work at the time of the survey. On the other hand, the difference between those who reported better health and those who reported worse health was surprisingly small in respect to time spent in other major activities, with the exception of volunteer service. Those who reported their health to be worse than expected reported a sharp decline in the amount of time spent in volunteer service. While more than one out of ten of the respondents whose health improved reported spending ten or more hours per week in volun-

---

*One of the findings of the study called *Aging in America, Trials and Triumphs* was that "health, wealth and an equally healthy spouse were found to be the major variables that determine happiness" (New York: Research and Forecast, Inc., 1980).

teer service, only about one in twenty-five of those whose health was worse than expected spent that much time in this activity.

The most clearcut relationship between response to a health-related question and postretirement experience was revealed by the respondents' answers to a question asking them to compare their health status to that of people their own age. The relationship between postretirement work experience and a perception that one's health is better than that of others one's own age is striking. Almost one out of three of the respondents who perceived that their health was better than their fellows had worked during retirement. Moreover, almost one out of five reported either working most of the time or almost every month. In contrast, only about one in seven of the respondents who reported that their health was worse than others of their own age had any work experience, and only one out of sixteen reported either working most months or almost every month. Almost as striking is the difference between those who reported that their health was better than others their own age and those who reported that it was the same. Only one out of twelve of the latter group reported working either most months or about every month.

The reason for this relationship between a perception of better health than others one's age and work after retirement is intriguing. It is by no means evident in which direction the causal relationship runs. It seems plausible that perceived health is the causal agent; but it may also be true of some, perhaps of many, of the respondents, that an active worklife after retirement leads them to conclude that they must be healthier than their peers who are not as actively engaged in work. And of course it is possible that postretirement work often makes an individual healthier than he would otherwise be. Such indeed is the conviction of many of the respondents who have worked during retirement. Our respondents made it abundantly clear that poor health not only added to financial burdens, but that it often contributed to boredom in retirement, since keeping active became more difficult and retirees with poorer health became tired of not doing very much with their time.

Alex worked for 12 years as a salesman before retiring in 1975 at the age of 51. He had been sick on and off for two years before his retirement and the pressures of work were increasing. His health qualified him for Social Security disability benefits, and his supervisor suggested that Chain Store could no longer keep him. He did not know in advance that he was going to retire and believes he retired too soon. In addition to his health problems are the financial difficulties brought by inflation and the feeling of being useless because he is not working. He feels that he does not have enough to do with his time. He expected retirement to be a largely unpleasant experience and it turned out even worse than he had expected. He has looked for work over the past few years but finds that companies feel he is a poor risk, because of his health. The drugs he is taking cause side effects, and he cannot get insurance. "You are a thing of the past," he complains. "No one cares if you are around or not."

Social Problems

Social life proved to be another area more pleasant than expected for most people and, in particular, for Chain Store men and Utility women. Nonetheless, the best social adjustment to retirement seemed to have been made by Utility men, and the worst by Manufacturer men, two in five of whom found their social lives less satisfying than they had anticipated. Utility men were least apt to report such problems as "not enough friends or social life," "not enough to do with my time," and "feel useless because not working." The fact that one in five Utility men and one in four Manufacturer men complain about spending too much time on home maintenance may be the result of a social problem: the wives of blue-collar workers with manual skills pressuring them to do things about the house.

Manufacturer men, more than other men, report that they feel useless because they are not working. Almost one in five complain that they do not have enough friends or social life, a complaint in line with the disappointment they voiced when comparing their postretirement experience with their expectations about social life. It would seem that for Manufacturer men in particular, the workplace not only gave meaning and structure to their lives, but provided important social bonds as well.

Manufacturer women also complained more than other women about not having enough friends or social life, but in other areas of social adjustment they did not vary much from the others of their own sex. Like Utility women, few (one in ten) felt useless because they were not working. For them, "had worked long enough" was a strong reason for having taken early retirement which they felt they had well earned. More Chain Store women than any others, however, felt they did not have enough to do with their time, and one in five—the largest number of any group—felt useless because they were not working.

As retirees began to spend more time at home, marital strains would frequently develop that could be covered over when more time was spent out of the house, away from the marital partner. This would often result in one spouse seeking activities outside the home, in order to avoid strain. One retiree characterized her relationship with her husband as being good because he went fishing daily. Another figured that, because of his nagging wife, he "might as well die working, instead of being at home." Jokingly, another commented, "Even if your wife adores you, she can't tolerate a foreign body 24 hours a day."

Sometimes, however, an equivalent, if not greater, amount of sorrow stemmed from the loneliness of not having a life partner as one grew older. One retiree pleaded for the "abolishment of stupid social and religious laws that keep men and women apart." He argued that "humans have a greater need for love and affection in old age." "Being alone is not good for anyone," agreed a respondent who had separated from her husband. Another woman, aged 55, abandoned by her husband, and struggling on a $280 Social Security disability check, asked, "Where do people under 65 on fixed incomes go for legal help?" For another respondent, a serious problem in retirement is not having enough contact with her children and other members of her family. She is lonely and would like to see more affordable private communities of retirees. "There are many people who don't have the means to live alone and are kicked out by their children," she writes. "We no longer send oldsters to the poor house, we just hope they die and the sooner, the better."

Although we have concentrated on individual problems for the sake of analytical simplicity, the existence of interrelatedness among the various problems and of the complexity of these relations should not be underestimated. Table 5.2 indicates, for example, that "own health" as a problem is interrelated with other major problems, particularly spouse's health, but somewhat less with inflation. Fears about personal safety were voiced by about one in five in the whole sample, almost as much by men as by women. Difficulties with transportation—lack of public transport, the high cost of operating and maintaining a car—were also mentioned by one in five. These two problems interacted with other problems, diminishing the possibilities of travel, of social life, and of filling one's time.

A 1981 national survey of a sample of persons older than 65 con-

Table 5.2 Interaction Among Problems: Cross-Tabulation of Major Problems Encountered During Retirement by Major Problems Encountered During Retirement (in percentages) (N=815)

Major problems encountered during retirement	(1) Inflation	(2) Trans-portation	(3) Own health	(4) Spouse's health	(5) Lack of friends and/ or contact with family	(6) Not enough to do and/ or feeling useless
Inflation	100.0	21.8	38.3	29.3	17.4	15.2
Transportation	93.8	100.0	43.8	29.2	21.9	10.1
Own health	91.6	24.4	100.0	35.3	20.6	16.6
Spouse's health	91.4	21.2	46.1	100.0	17.1	13.1
Lack of friends and/or contact	92.4	27.1	45.8	29.2	100.0	22.2
Not enough to do and/or feeling useless	93.5	14.5	42.7	25.8	25.8	100.0

cluded that many popular perceptions about the problems of this group were "myths" and that

> On the impact of inflation, coping with energy, loneliness, poor health, fear of crime, poor housing, not enough job opportunities, not enough medical care, getting transportation to stores, to doctors, to recreation—on all of these, much larger numbers of the nonelderly are convinced older people are in more desperate shape than the elderly themselves report they are.*

For two in three of our respondents, retirement, as was indicated, was indeed a pleasant experience. These respondents had, however, been attached for most of their worklives to what labor economists call the "primary" labor market, working for large and stable corporations, earning relatively good wages, owning their own homes in most cases, and collecting company pensions as well as social security. This combination of favorable circumstances is not characteristic of all members of these same age groups. A considerable fraction, among whom are to be found some members of minority groups, some unattached women, many of the physically or mentally handicapped, and workers with irregular and/or low-paying work histories, are much less fortunate. Furthermore, one in three of our respondents, a not-insignificant fraction, found themselves saddled with problems whose seriousness and intractability made their retirement far less pleasant than they had anticipated.

It is of some interest, however, that the oldest respondents in the survey, those 65 and older, were much more apt to report general satisfaction with retirement. Not only did more of them expect that retirement would be very pleasant, they were also much more likely to say that their retirement experience had met their expectation. They also reported more frequently that their health, compared to others their age, was better.

These attitudes were expressed despite the fact that the proportion of respondents whose total family income is $15,000 or less increased with the age of the respondents at the time of the survey, from about 60 percent of the 55–59 and 60–64 age groups to about 80 percent of those 65 and older. Even though their incomes were relatively low, their general state of satisfaction, their health, and their activity levels compare very favorably with the younger age groups. Since those respondents who are relatively older are also apt to be those who retired relatively later (or were mandatorily re-

*Louis Harris, *New York Times*, November 19, 1981, A18.

tired), here again is confirmation of the fact that comparatively early retirement, although very satisfactory for a large proportion of those who chose it, was also more frequently associated with health problems and unsatisfactory work situations. Moreover, even though their comparative income situation is more favorable, respondents in the younger age groups tend to express feelings of being under more economic pressure. They also tend to be less satisfied with their income levels.

It may be that these younger respondents felt more anxiety about prospects of continued inflation because they looked forward to more years of increasingly severe inflationary pressures upon their relatively inflexible income. To the extent that their company pensions and other retirement assets represented a higher proportion of their total income, these younger retirees were of course less protected by the indexing of Social Security benefits.

The Timing of the Retirement Decision

Knowing what retirement was like, how, in retrospect, did the respondents feel about the timing of their retirement decision? The overwhelming number, from three-fourths to nine-tenths of the individual groups, felt they had made the right decision and had retired at the right time, or had even waited too long and had retired too late.

On the other hand, some felt they had retired too soon. The largest number who expressed this opinion—one in four—consisted of Chain Store women, closely followed by Chain Store men and Manufacturer women (one in five of each). One in seven of Utility men and women and of Manufacturer men also felt this way.

There are no surprises in the identity of those who voiced these sentiments most strongly. Chain Store women, more than other women, felt useless, with not enough to do with their time, and also complained more about having too little contact with family members. In comparing preretirement expectations with postretirement realities, they were the most seriously disappointed with their postretirement incomes. Similarly, Chain Store men complained more than any other group about not being able to fill their time and also had serious concerns about the feeling of uselessness induced by not working. Both these groups had also indicated in larger number than the average that they had found retirement less satisfactory than anticipated.

Manufacturer women had earned the least before retirement, had felt inflation more keenly, and had been forced to make a "large" response to inflationary pressures in greater numbers than any other group. Finally, a fair number of them, like the Manufacturer men, found a void in their social lives. Where the workplace provided both income and social life, retiring "too soon" becomes a predictable reaction.

Possible Changes in Retirement Timing

Since the conditions that might lead to either earlier or later retirement are of obvious importance from an individual, business, and public standpoint, the respondents were asked to indicate what changes in company policy might have altered the timing of their retirement decisions.

It is clear from Table 5.3 that more than half of all respondents except Manufacturer and Chain Store women believed that neither the hindsight gained from experiencing retirement nor changes in company policy would have induced them to retire earlier. The same was true of more than two in five of the other women as well. The proposed company policy which seemed to evoke the strongest positive response, particularly by Utility retirees, was one that would have permitted contributions to increase the size of the pension. One in sixteen Utility retirees also favored a policy of company recall of retirees for temporary work.

A smaller number of each group indicated that *no* change in company policy would have caused them to retire *later*. The strongest resistance was registered by Utility retirees. Utility men in largest number cited the pressures of work as a reason for retirement, and Utility women "had worked long enough." Manufacturer and Chain Store women on the other hand seemed the most responsive to the idea of retiring later. The changes in company policy that seemed most likely to induce later retirement included flexible work schedules and/or reduced hours for older workers; better chances for older workers to earn promotions and/or increases in wages; and job reassignments that reduced the pressure of work. Since it was possible for the same respondent to indicate conditions both for retiring earlier *and* later, a summary of all possible responses is shown in Table 5.4. From these responses it is evi-

Table 5.3 Possible Changes in Retirement Timing (responses
as percentage of respondents)

Conditions	Males			Females		
	Util.	Mfg.	Chain Store	Util.	Mfg.	Chain Store
Retire earlier						
1. If company had						
not offered raise/ promotion to delay retirement	1	1	5	3	2	4
permitted me to make contribu- tions to increase pension	16	8	6	12	4	2
policy of recalling retired for temporary work	6	4	4	6	4	5
2. If I had known what retirement would be like	9	7	6	6	4	6
3. None of the above	59	53	58	59	45	47
Retire later						
1. If company had offered older workers						
flexible work schedules/reduced hours	13	8	14	8	6	11
better chances for promotion	15	4	8	11	8	9
job reassignments that reduced pressure	13	8	15	7	6	14
retraining	4	1	3	4	2	4
retirement at age 70, not 65	13	11	13	8	8	16
strong anti-age discrimination policy	8	4	6	9	2	8
2. If I had known what retirement would be like	7	1	5	6	2	5
3. None of above	49	48	42	51	36	37

Table 5.4 Summary: Possible Changes in Retirement Timing
(in percentages)

Responses to possible changes in company policy	Males			Females		
	Util.	Mfg.	Chain Store	Util.	Mfg.	Chain Store
Retire earlier, not later	8	11	7	9	10	11
Retire later, not earlier	20	18	25	11	18	26
Might retire either earlier or later	24	15	16	18	12	16
No change	48	56	52	62	60	46
Total	100	100	100	100	100	100

dent that no change in company policy would have altered the decisions of about half the male respondents nor of an even larger number—three in five—of the Utility and Manufacturer women. These respondents seemed convinced that, all things considered, they had retired at the right time.

Of those who would have considered a change, more say that they would have retired later, rather than earlier. About one in five of the total (except for the Utility women) would have made such a decision. When the two groups who, given certain company policies, might have decided to retire either earlier or later are added to those who indicated that, under certain conditions, they might have retired *either* earlier *or* later, it seems that changes in company policy would have affected the timing of the retirement decision of slightly less than half the respondents. Chain Store women, Utility men, and Chain Store men, in that order, were particularly responsive to the possibility of change.

Reflections About Aging

The retirees who responded to our questionnaire had many thoughts, both positive and negative, about the aging process itself. Many believed that they were in the special position of having the time to do the things everyone wanted to do. "As soon as you feel too old to do something, do it," wrote one retiree. "Live so you wouldn't be ashamed to sell your parrot to the town gossip." One retiree felt particularly sorry for the white-collar worker who, he felt, was at more of a disadvantage than the blue-collar worker as he got older. "I pity the white-collar worker," he wrote, "who in particular industries must be a Madison Avenue image. They look for youth and it's phony, but that's America." Retirement was viewed to mean freedom from commuting, watching a time clock, and taking orders from a boss, but not necessarily from activity and exploration. "I retired from a job," noted one retiree, "not from living and learning new things." And, in the words of another retiree who believes age is all in the mind, "Some people of 50 are older in their habits than others are at 65."

On the other hand, many retirees expressed a great fear of aging, particularly as it meant a potential decline in health and ability to be active and an increase in medical bills. "Almost all retirees live in fear of the day they may wake up and find they've had a stroke," wrote one retiree, and in the words of another, "The man who said the last half is best was crazy as hell." "My first advice to anyone would be to be active in other things as well as their jobs," wrote one woman, a retiree from Utility. "Men especially devote their lives to their work and when that is no longer available their lives are abruptly changed and they feel lost. I've seen so many. The word itself, 'retirement', seems to frighten many people. Rather than looking at it as another change in life style, they see it as the end of living and enjoying, a time of boredom and idleness."

The retirees in our survey, then, had a full range of experiences and feeling about retirement: from bitterness to extreme satisfaction, from relative inactivity to the opening of new vistas, from pessimism about the future to optimism about where their lives were taking them. Some were working for pay, many were not. Some were in very poor health, others were not. Many had severe financial difficulties; some, able to get by on less or having been able throughout their lives to accumulate more, did not.

CHAPTER 6

What Difference Did Gender Make? Or the Company One Kept?

In the earlier analysis of the preretirement experiences of professional and supervisory personnel of three large companies, women constituted too small a part of the group—less than 5 percent—to make their experiences, however interesting, the basis of any extensive generalizations.

In this analysis of retired nonsupervisory employees of these same companies, however, almost half the sample—388 out of a total of 840—were women. So large a number can no longer be treated as an anomaly; the experiences of these women command both analytic respectability and social interest. In this chapter some aspects of the retirement experience will be reviewed in terms of gender, more specifically, gender by company affiliation, since the latter also introduces significant variations.

An analysis of sex distribution by company reveals a rough numerical balance among Chain Store respondents (188 men, 177 women). The Utility sample was somewhat more skewed toward women (158 women, 121 men), while the sex distribution among Manufacturer's respondents was heavily male (143), with only one in four (53) of the respondents women. Chain Store female respondents made up 46 percent of all women in the sample, Utility 41 percent, and Manufacturing, which had both the smallest number of respondents and the smallest number of women, only 14 percent.

Demographic Profile

MARITAL STATUS BEFORE AND AFTER RETIREMENT

Before retirement, nine out of ten male respondents were married, but the same was true of only three out of five of the women respondents. While one man in 27 was widowed, widowhood was the lot of one in five of the women. More women, proportionately, were also divorced or separated—one in eleven—than men (one in 37). Finally, 12 percent of the women had never been married, while such a description applied to only one man in 37. In sum, "divorced," "separated," and "never married" described one in six of the women but only one in twenty of the men.

One can only speculate about the reasons for the disparity in marital status among the male and female respondents. Aside from the fact that for a single woman, earning one's own livelihood could obviously be essential, it is not clear how the causal arrow points between work and a woman's marital status. Perhaps the more pertinent question is how it was possible for three out of five women of this generation to combine marriage (and in some cases, children) with lengthy work commitments in an era inhospitable to the participation of married women in the labor force.

Marital status after retirement revealed the inevitable inroads of time with an increase in the number of the widowed among both men and women. Not surprisingly, this increase was larger for women (almost 10 percentage points) than for men (4 percentage points). As a consequence, 87 percent of the men but only one-half of the women described themselves as "married" at the time of the survey. Almost one woman in three was widowed, but only one man in 13 was in the same situation.

MARITAL STATUS BY COMPANY

Company affiliation reveals a fair degree of diversity in the marital status of women employees when considered by company, but far more uniformity among the men.

Before retirement, women working for Chain Store had the highest proportion of "married" (almost two in three) and the lowest proportion of "divorced/separated" and "never married". In contrast, women employees of Manufacturer had the smallest share of "married" (only one in two) and the largest share of "never married." The women who had worked for Utility had almost as high a marriage rate as Chain Store women, a far lower rate of widowhood, but the largest share of "divorced/separated" and almost as large a share of "never married" as Manufacturer.

Once retired, Manufacturer women who had been married suffered the highest rate of widowhood, reducing their already low share of the "married" from one in two to two in five; Chain Store married women, on the other hand, had the lowest rate of marital attrition.

Of some interest is the fact that retirees of Chain Store, women and men alike, had the highest share of "married" and the lowest share of both "divorced/separated" and "never married," while male and female employees of Manufacturer had both the lowest marriage rate and the highest rate of widowhood after retirement.

AGE AT RETIREMENT

About 70 percent of the women and 65 percent of the men had retired by age 62 or younger. In fact, one-third of the women and one-quarter of the men had retired by age 59. While relatively more women than men took early retirement, virtually identical proportions of both sexes—one in five—retired at ages 62 and 65. The mean age at retirement for men was 60.8 years and for women, 60.38.

Early retirement among women employees of Utility far exceeded these norms. Almost one-half had retired by age 59 and only one in four worked past the age of 62. Their mean age at retirement was a full year younger than the average. Their male coworkers also exceeded the male norm for early retirement, with almost one in three retiring before age 60. But unlike the women workers, they exceeded the norm at the other end of the scale as well, registering the largest share of men—two in five—retiring between the ages of 63 and 65.

One-third of Manufacturer women had retired by age 59, and by age 62 three in four had left the company. In contrast, only one in ten of Manufacturer male retirees—by far the smallest share—took retirement before age 60. For the men, retirement took place largely between the ages of 60 and 62. The mean age of the men, 61.5, exceeded the sample average, while the reverse was true for the women.

The age distribution of Chain Store employees provided some interesting reversals between the male and female norms. Only one in five of the women, but one in three of the men, retired by age 59. Not only did fewer Chain Store women elect early retirement than the other women in the sample, but two in five, by far the largest share for all women, took retirement only when mandated.* As a consequence, their mean age was more than a full year above the average for women.

PRESENT AGE

At the time the survey was taken, the mean age of the men was 67.3 years and of the women, 66.7. Chain Store women and Manufacturer men were older than average, while Utility retirees of both sexes were somewhat younger. In fact, one Utility retiree in seven was younger than 60, and this company's respondents had the smallest representation in the over-70 age group. Two in five of the Manufacturer male retirees, in contrast, were in this oldest group, as was one in three of the Chain Store women.

EDUCATION

When educational attainment is divided into three levels—less than 12 years schooling, 12 years (high school diploma), and more than 12 years—about the same proportion of men and women overall, two in five, were found to have had less than 12 years of formal schooling. Beyond that level, however, male and female educational paths diverged. Women were more likely to have been high school graduates than men (44% compared to 33%), but less likely to have gone beyond high school than their male co-workers (15% compared to 24%).

Analysis by company introduces additional differentiation for men and women. Chain Store employees of both sexes had the highest levels of educational attainment, with two in three of the women and an even higher percentage of the men having completed at least 12 years of schooling. Further, male Chain Store employees had the largest share (36%) of post-secondary school education of any group in the sample. In the cases of Utility and Manufacturer, the women employees had basically similar educational distributions, close to the average for all women described

---

*For part of the period covered, mandatory retirement age in this company was below age 65.

above. The male retirees of Manufacturer, however, were more concentrated at the lower end of the educational scale than their counterparts at Utility; more than half the Utility men had completed 12 years or more of schooling compared with only two in five of Manufacturer men.

Supplementary exposure to vocational training was also mentioned by three in five of the men and two in five of the women.

More than half the Utility men mentioned "company school" as a source of training; about two in five, noncompany schools; somewhat over one in three, military service; and one in four, apprenticeship. For the men affiliated with the other two companies, noncompany schools were more important sources of vocational training, cited by three in five of the Manufacturer men and two in five of the Chain Store men. In the case of this last group, military service was mentioned more frequently (by almost half the group) than any other single source of training. Apprenticeship as a source of training was more important for Manufacturer men (two in five) than for any other single group.

Noncompany schools were the major sources of vocational training for the women: three in four of Chain Store women and one in two of the women in the other two companies mentioned these in their responses. Two women mentioned the military as a source and another handful, apprenticeship; but the only source of any significance other than noncompany schools was the company school, mentioned by two in five of both Utility and Manufacturer women and one in three of Chain Store women.

Economic Profile

YEARS WORKED FOR THE COMPANY

Most respondents, men and women alike, were long-term employees. The men had worked on average 28.5 years and the women 25.5 years for the same company. More than one-half the men and almost one-third of the women had worked more than 30 years for the company from which they retired. One in seven of the men had worked 40 years or more, virtually the whole of their adult lives, for the same company.

The phenomenon of life-long company affiliation is most visible among Utility employees. Four in five of the men and over one-half of the women had worked at least 30 years, and one in three of the men and one in seven of the women, 40 years or more for Utility. In fact, *no* Utility respondent, male or female, had worked fewer than ten years for the company, and only *one in one hundred* had worked fewer than 20 years.

At the other extreme, there were few Chain Store respondents to be found with 40-year work careers, and the number who had worked 30 years was below the sample average. The largest number of both sexes had worked between 20 and 29 years for the company.

Manufacturer employees occupied middle ground, close in most respects to the average for the whole group. They had longer work affiliations than was the case with Chain Store but did not have the extraordinarily lengthy job tenures of Utility workers.

OCCUPATIONAL DISTRIBUTION

The jobs performed during these long worklives can be described generally as nonprofessional and nonmanagerial and concentrated in the blue-collar, sales, and clerical categories. More specific dimensions of these jobs can be established by use of the schema developed in an earlier Conservation of Human Resources analysis of job training outlined in Chapter 1.

Taken together, almost one-half of the men in the panel had held semiskilled jobs of the type listed in Class 5, while more than one-half of the women had been employed in low-skill clerical jobs for which training is usually received on the job (Class 6). When the relatively small number of women who had held the higher-level clerical jobs for which pre-employment training *is* required—the secretaries and typists of Class 2—are taken into account, more than three out of five women were found to have held clerical jobs. Similarly, when the high-skill blue-collar jobs of Class 4 and the low-skill blue-collar jobs of Class 7 are added together, more than three out of four men held blue-collar jobs of varying degrees of skill. Not unexpectedly, neither the high-skill white-collar occupations of Class 3 nor the low-skill service occupations of Class 8 have any sizable representation. One in six of both sexes, however, are classified as "managers and supervisors" (Class 9). These were usually foremen in Utility and Manufacturer or section heads in Chain Store.

The occupational distributions within individual companies exhibit some interesting deviations from the average. Nine out of ten male respondents of both Utility and Manufacturer held blue-collar jobs, rather evenly distributed among Classes 4, 5, and 7 in the case of Manufacturer and largely concentrated in Class 5 in the case of Utility. On the other hand, almost one in two of Chain Store men were salesmen and thus classified in Class 5, while another one-third gave job descriptions that indicated at least modest levels of managerial capacity, thus placing them in Class 9.

One in two of the women employees of Chain Store had held low-level sales and clerical positions (Class 6). Traditionally, few women are given the opportunity to acquire the knowledge of the product required to sell "big ticket" items. These are usually handled by sales*men*, rather than by sales*clerks*; the latter are usually female, handle simpler products, and are lower paid. On the other hand, more than one in four of Chain Store women had been in charge of at least small sales divisions and were thus classified as managers (Class 9).

In the case of Utility women, about three out of four had held low-level clerical jobs, while the second largest concentration—one in five—was found in such jobs as "service representative" which, since they require more than three-months training on the job, are classified as Class 5 occupations.

Manufacturer women had an occupational distribution different from that of the women in the other two companies. By far the largest number, two out of five, had been low-skill blue-collar operatives (Class 7). Of the clericals, more than half held jobs requiring the pre-employment training which placed them in Class 2.

Earnings: Adjusted Hourly Wage Rates

Regardless of the differences in their occupational distributions, women generally held the lower-paying jobs in each of the three companies.

After hourly pay before retirement was adjusted to 1979 price levels, the following general findings emerged:

  the mean adjusted hourly wage rate for men was $9.06 and for women, $6.16;
  20 percent of the women, on average, earned less than $5.00 per hour, but only 2 percent of the men;
  about nine out of ten of the women earned $7.50 per hour or less;
  two in three of the men earned more than $7.50 per hour, but only one woman in six.

Utility men were at the highest end of the wage scale. They had the highest mean hourly wage rate ($10.04); almost three in five earned $7.50 per hour or more, and one in four earned between

$10 and $12.49 per hour. These last rates translate into yearly earnings (adjusted to the 1979 price level) of between $20,800 and almost $26,000 per year. The mean hourly wage rates of Manufacturer and Chain Store men were close at about $8.70, some 13 percent lower than the Utility rate.

Utility women ranked lower on the pay scale than their male coworkers but, like them, were the best paid of their own sex. They had the highest female mean wage ($6.84 per hour). Three in five earned between $5 and $7.50 per hour (between $10,400 and $15,600 per year), and one in five—a considerably larger share than for the other two groups of women—was in the next higher wage bracket. The mean wage rate of Manufacturer women was almost 10 percent less ($6.24). Three in four earned between $5 and $7.50 per hour and, while not as well paid as Utility women, were better off than the Chain Store women who, with a mean wage rate of $5.64 per hour, were the lowest paid in the sample. Nine out of ten of these women earned $7.50 or less, and they had the largest representation in the "below $5" class.*

The disparity between male and female wage rates is apparent. The mean hourly wage rate of the lower-paid women was two-thirds that of the lowest-paid men, and even the highest-paid Utility women received only three-quarters of the lowest-average male wage rate.

How did women perceive the quality of their work situation and their status as lower-paid members of the workforce? Both the number and tenor of the written comments are revealing. Several expressed their resentment at age discrimination on the part of management in the later years of their employment. A secretary who had worked for Chain Store for 28 years felt that

> Older, but experienced and conscientious, people are not given a chance for promotion. Also the older people have to take orders from the younger and inexperienced personnel, which gives one an inferior feeling.
>
> I did *not want to retire.* I was in good health, had a good position, good coworkers, and was happy. Of course I couldn't get a promotion because of my age although I knew the job very well. They put in a young girl as an assistant to my superior, and I had to take orders from her which I resented, and I then asked for a transfer to another department.

*Response rates to this question were lowest for Utility women (54%) and Chain Store men (57%). Utility women who were on salary and Chain Store men who were on commissions probably had difficulty in answering a question on hourly wage rates.

Since such comments were also made by the men, they did not reflect perceptions originating in sex differences. More interesting is the fact that of the 388 women in the sample, *only two,* both, as it happens, employees of Chain Store, voiced complaints about sex discrimination.

A furniture salesperson for more than 27 years claimed:

I could work rings around the young men in my department. Instead of promotions I trained all of the Div. Mgrs. for years. Also moved Furniture—did all display in Dept.
Not complaining—I liked it—helped me do a better selling job.

A telephone department supervisor for 23 years complained:

When I was working, they didn't pay women enough even tho they did the same work as men. I draw a very small SS pension. I was good at my job. I also sold, as well as being over telephone service. I have had letters of recommendation when I worked.

It would seem that in the case of both Manufacturer and Utility the nature of the product made occupational segregation seem altogether natural. Traditionally, skilled blue-collar jobs were male, clerical and low-level sales and operative jobs, female. Only in the case of Chain Store, where there was some overlap of function in the sales area, was there some questioning of the usual hierarchical arrangements.

Women's lower hourly pay and lifetime earnings are usually regarded as a function of their preference for part-time work and an irregular attachment to the labor market. The women in the sample, however, had had almost lifetime attachments to their company on a full-time basis. Occupational segregation and restricted promotional paths were more likely explanations of inferior financial status than lack of work commitment or of loyalty to the firm.

ADJUSTED TOTAL FAMILY INCOME

Family income provides a more comprehensive indicator of economic well-being than do wage rates, reflecting not only nonwage sources of income but, in some cases, the contributions of two-worker families. Data were obtained on total family income in the year before retirement, including own earnings, spouse's earnings and/or pension, income from investments or rental property, and all other sources, and were adjusted to 1979 price levels.

as the case with wage rates, men were a more-favored group ☐ndicator of total family income than the women. Only one ☐ six reported total family income of less than $15,000, compared with two in five of the women. Half the men were in the $15,000 to $25,000 range, but fewer than one woman in three. One in three of the men reported total family income of $25,000 or more; one in five of the total (included in this last group) were in the $30,000 and over group. This was the only part of the income scale where there was some convergence of female with male total income.

The highest mean income for own sex was reported by Chain Store employees, both male and female (both of whom, aside from other sources of income, had the possiblity of earning commissions), the lowest by Manufacturer. Manufacturer women had the lowest total family income in the sample, more than half reporting a total income of less than $15,000. Here, marital status is a possible explanatory factor since, with only one in two married before retirement, the possibility of two-worker sources of income was obviously limited.

While Manufacturer men reported higher family incomes than the women, like them they lagged behind retirees of the same sex from the other two companies. Almost three in four of both Chain Store and Utility men were in the $20,000 and over class, but fewer than one out of two Manufacturer men. The last also had minimal representation—only one in nine—in the $30,000 and over category, compared with one in four of the Chain Store men and one in five of Utility men.

Chain Store women had the highest mean income among the women ($23,015), but a distribution among income categories which was largely bimodal. Forty-three percent were in the $15,000 and under class, and 29 percent in the $25,000 and over group. Utility women, in contrast, had a more-uniform income distribution, with about one in three found in each of the three merged income groups, $15,000 and under, $15,000 to $25,000, and $25,000 and over. They also had the highest representation— almost one in four—in the highest income class ($30,000 and over).

The Retirement Decision

REASONS FOR RETIREMENT

With the exclusion of 199 respondents who gave "reached mandatory retirement" as a reason for retirement, the analysis was focused on the 641 respondents who had elected retirement and their reasons for this decision (Table 6.1).*

As a preliminary, it should be noted that a total of 851 responses were given by 348 men, and 597 responses, by 293 women. The number of responses, together with the write-in comments, makes it clear that most respondents had more than one reason for taking early retirement. These may by categorized from a variety of perspectives:

> Some reflect monetary incentives, both positive and negative, such as "could afford to," "did not pay to work," "received an attractive pension offer," "received disability benefits."
>
> Some indicate a health condition which made it either necessary or desirable to retire. The actual receipt of disability benefits (from the company, social security, or both) both facilitated retirement for health reasons and provided objective evidence of the seriousness of this reason.
>
> A third category reflects dissatisfaction with the work situation; with the pressures of work; with perceived hostile or unfair treatment by managers, supervisors, or fellow workers; and includes a general, catch-all conclusion—"worked long enough."
>
> The fourth and last category consists of "retirement was suggested" or an actual lay-off (because of plant relocation). This category was quantitatively not significant.

It is clear that other combinations were possible, including one that distinguished between objective, verifiable reasons, of which there are only two—received disability benefits and plant lay-off—and subjective reasons, which make up the balance of the list. More significant than the classification scheme used is recognition of the interactive nature of the reasons underlying decisions to take early retirement. One of many possible negative scenarios includes perceived job pressures, poor treatment by supervisors, a resultant deterioration in health status, the conclusion that one has worked long enough, it does not pay to work, etc.

For men, poor health was the primary reason for taking early retirement, cited by almost one in two, regardless of company affiliation. The receipt of disability benefits by more than one-quarter of the men gives objective verification of the significance of this factor. Two in five of the men indicated they could afford to retire,

---

*There were actually 202 respondents who were mandatorily retired, but three cases with missing information on company were excluded. Of the total sample of 849 cases, 641 usable cases of early retirement are analyzed in this chapter.

Table 6.1 Reasons for Early Retirement by Sex and Company, Responses as Percentage of Respondents (N=641)

| | Company-Sex | | | | | | Responses: 348 males, 293 females | | | | |
| | Utility | | Manufac-turer | | Chain Store | | | | | | |
Reason	M	F	M	F	M	F	Males	% all Males	Females	% all Females	Total N
1. Could afford	40	40	26	23	53	29	144	41	96	33	240
Not pay to work	23	14	18	5	9	9	54	15	31	11	85
Attractive pension offer	5	15	19	21	7	2	35	10	31	11	66
2. Health	43	18	46	37	46	39	157	45	81	27	238
Received disability	24	13	30	23	27	15	94	27	44	15	138
3. Pressure	32	25	17	16	37	31	102	29	76	26	178

Table 6.1 Continued

Responses: 348 males, 293 females

| | Company-Sex | | | | | | | % all | | % all | Total |
| | Utility | | Manufac-turer | | Chain Store | | | Males | | Females | N |
	M	F	M	F	M	F	Males	Males	Females	Females	
Treatment of older workers	44	32	22	33	30	31	109	31	93	32	202
Worked long enough	41	45	37	42	27	37	119	34	121	41	240
4. Retirement suggested	7	6	10	2	10	8	30	9	18	6	48
Laid off	1	2	4	2	1	1	7	2	6	2	13
Total respondents	94	126	107	43	147	124	851		597		1,448
	220		150		271						

Note: Respondents who checked "mandatory retirement" are not included in the table. Since respondents could check more than one reason for retirement, the sum of the percentage distributions exceeds 100.

but here company differentials become significant. More than half the Chain Store men and two in five of the Utility men gave this reason, but only one in four of the Manufacturer men.

The responses of Utility men reveal a pattern of psychological duress: treatment of older workers by managers, supervisors, and co-workers ranks first, even ahead of health, as a reason to take early retirement; "worked long enough" is more important to them than to the other men in the sample; and for one in three, "pressure of work" was also given as a reason. While even more Chain Store men cited pressure as a reason for early retirement, the other two indicators of duress were not nearly as significant.

For the women in the sample, the most important reason for retiring was the feeling that they had worked long enough: they were tired of "getting up at 5:30 am to shovel snow and drive 30 miles to work." As for the men, "could afford to" was overall the second most important reason to retire. As large a share of Utility women cited this reason as did Utility men, but it was less important a reason to Manufacturer women than to their male co-workers, and far less so to Chain Store women compared with Chain Store men (53% opposed to 29%).

While poor health as a reason for retirement ranked first for the men, it was a far less important reason for the women. The size of the sex differential is striking in this instance: 45 percent of the men but only 27 percent of the women indicated that this was an initiating factor. Fewer than half the Utility women cited this reason, as did their male co-workers, and women in the other two companies also ranked these significantly lower than the men in the same companies.

Not unexpectedly, the availability of disability benefits was cited by almost twice as many men as women as a reason for retirement. Employees in Manufacturer, men and women alike, had the largest shares in this category. Unlike the usual very early retirees among our respondents, Utility women who had retired at such ages had the lowest representation in the health and health-related categories.

Although Utility men had the sharpest perceptions of age discrimination, one in three of all women respondents and one in four of the men affiliated with the other two companies also gave the treatment of older workers as a reason for retirement. Only 4 percent of the respondents singled out their co-workers as being at fault, but about one in six of Utility and Manufacturer women and of all Chain Store employees blamed managers, and about one in ten singled out supervisors as well.

Planning for Retirement

RETIREMENT TIMING

To the extent that advance knowledge about the date of retirement is an indicator of planning, men seemed to engage in somewhat longer-range planning for retirement than women. A larger share of men than women in all three companies knew more than three years in advance when they would retire. On the other hand, one in four of men and women alike knew the date of their retirement less than three months in advance; Chain Store women are overrepresented on this short end of the planning time scale.

VOLUNTARY DELAY OF RETIREMENT

The need to support children or other family members can act to delay retirement, but for most sample members this was an inconsequential factor except for Utility women, one in six of whom indicated that they had delayed their retirement for such reasons.

INFLUENCE OF THE WORK STATUS OF THE SPOUSE IN PLANNING RETIREMENT

Since the receipt of either wage or pension income by the spouse can affect the retirement decision, respondents were asked to indicate which of various possibilities reflected their own situation.

The following picture emerged for the men:

Two in three of the men in all three companies indicated that their wives were *not* employed at the time they retired; one in four indicated that their wives had never worked.

Of those whose wives *were* employed at the time they retired:

More than half indicated they would have retired in any case. The largest number who had made such independent decisions—seven out of ten—were Chain Store men.

About two in five of Utility and Chain Store men had made joint decisions with their wives to retire together. Only one in four of Manufacturer men reported such arrangements.

For two in five of Manufacturer men and one in three of Chain Store men, the continued employment of their wives made their own retirement possible. For Utility men this was a less important factor.

The wife of about one retiree in eleven in each of the companies delayed her own retirement when her husband retired.

One in six of the male retirees, regardless of company, indicated that "without two pensions, neither my spouse nor I could have afforded to retire."

Finally, one in six of Manufacturer and Chain Store men and one in ten of Utility men claimed that "my spouse and I have usually made our decision about working separately and that was the case with the decision to retire."

The summary picture that emerges from the men's responses is that the majority did not have wives who were working at the time they decided to retire but, for those who did, the continued employment of their wives and the availability of two pensions was of some significance in facilitating retirement in a fair number of cases.

In contrast, the husband's work/retirement status played a significantly larger role in determining the women's retirement decisions. Fewer than one in five, regardless of company, reported that decisions about work and retirement were made independent of the husband's decisions. The husbands of two in three of the Utility women, three in four of the Manufacturer women, and three in five of the Chain Store women were employed at the time they retired, a fact which presumably eased their way. Between 30 and 40 percent of the women whose husbands were working indicated there was a family agreement to retire together. Half of all Manufacturer women reported that two pensions were required to retire, as did two in five of the Utility women. Three in four of Chain Store women, on the other hand, indicated they were not faced with so compelling a consideration.

The Postretirement Work Decision

For men and women alike, the three most important problems after retirement were inflation, own health, and spouse's health. For women, the latter was of particular concern. Poor social adjustment and feeling useless was a problem mainly of Manufacturer men and Chain Store women. Returning to work after retirement provided one type of solution to these problems.

THE WORK RETURNERS

After retirement, about two hundred persons, almost one-quarter of the sample, had returned to paid work for some period of time ranging from "just about every month" to "most months" to "some months, but not very many." About half this number, or 12 percent of the sample, had been almost continuously employed since retirement. Most had held one job since retirement. A large number, about four out of five of these continuous workers, were currently employed at the time of the survey.

Chain Store men and women alike had reported in largest numbers that they had found their health after retirement better than that of others their age and had also expressed keen disappointment with many aspects of retirement. They were the most numerous among the work returners. Forty percent of the men and 22 percent of the women had worked some time since retirement. Half of these men in fact worked either "just about every month" or "most months," and the same was true of more than half the Chain Store women.

While only 14 percent of the Manufacturer women—the smallest number in the sample—had some postretirement work, more of them—10 percent—had worked every month than any other group except Chain Store men.

The smallest number of work returners came from the ranks of Utility men and women, both of whom had expressed the sharpest resentments of work pressures before retirement and had the fewest complaints about retirement.

Women as a whole stressed the social reasons for returns to work far more than did the men. Although Manufacturer women were forced to make "large" responses to economic pressures, they still gave greater emphasis to the social than to the economic reasons for going back to work; for Chain Store women, social reasons assumed the highest degree of importance.

In this chapter the retirement experience has been viewed in terms of both gender and of company affiliation. The introduction of these two dimensions reveals not only important differences in the retirement decisions and the postretirement experiences of both men and women (taking into account their company affiliations), but has also in some cases illuminated some of the relationships observed in the previous chapter.

To summarize: women were somewhat younger than the men at the time of retirement, were more likely to have been high school graduates but less likely to have some college education, and were married in fewer numbers than the men, both in the post-retirement period and at the time of the survey.

Like the men, most women were long-term employees. Utility women, who had retired at the youngest ages, also had the longest work careers of all the women in the sample (just as Utility men had of all the men). Chain Store women were older when they retired. They were most likely of all the women in the sample to be married, to have had more years of schooling, but also to have had shorter job tenures than either Utility or Manufacturer women.

In all three companies there was clear occupational segregation along sex lines. Utility and Manufacturer men held on the whole semiskilled blue-collar jobs, while Chain Store men were largely salesmen and in some cases section heads. Women in all three companies held largely low-skill clerical, operative, and sales jobs with their skills acquired mainly on the job. Their concentration in such jobs reflected occupational stereotyping rather than differences in educational levels. Women's jobs were on the whole the lowest-paying jobs in the organization, and their hourly wage rates when compared with the men's reflected faithfully the conventional ratio of women's to men's earnings of 60 percent. Women's total family incomes were also inferior to that of the men. This was particularly true for Manufacturer women, who had among their ranks the largest number of the unmarried.

The major reason given by the men for taking early retirement was poor health, with the exception of Utility men who reported in large numbers that the pressure of managers and supervisors upon older workers forced their retirement. For the women, the most important reason for retiring was they had "paid their dues" and worked long enough.

Retirement did not lead to any relative improvement in the financial status of the women. They had both lower total family incomes and lower total retirement benefits than the men. Neither was their family situation likely to compensate for their inferior economic status, since only one in two was married at the time of the survey, as contrasted with almost nine out of ten of the men.

The extraordinarily lengthy worklives of these nonprofessional women, so much at variance with the prevailing image of the home-bound women in the postwar decades, suggest that we are dealing with a neglected chapter in the social-industrial history of our times.

The important question that emerges is how the women in this study were able to combine lifetime work with home responsibilities in an era inhospitable in every way to such commitments. Neither the support systems nor the domestic task-sharing that contemporary women expect were prevailing norms. How, in short, did these women do it? What were their motivations? What would they have done differently?

Through additional research with the women in the sample, we hope to shed some light on these relatively unexplored areas.

CHAPTER 7

The Retirement Experience of Major Subgroups

One of the major purposes of this investigation of the workers who decided to retire before the normal retirement age has been to ascertain whether any significant changes have taken place since 1968 in the nature of the retirement decision and the character of postretirement experiences. Another major purpose was to compare those who elected early retirement with those who chose to work until they reached mandatory retirement age. In addition, we wished to be able to examine the experiences of retirees in different age groups.

Date of Retirement: The Vintages

We have grouped the respondents into two groups by date of retirement: those who retired between 1968 and 1972 and those who retired between 1973 and 1978. The panel from which the respondents came was structured to include an equal number of individuals who retired in each of the eleven years from 1968 through 1978. Because response rates varied by year of retirement, the actual proportions of respondents found in each of these two groups differs to some extent from what would have been the case if equal response rates had been obtained in each of these eleven years.

A partial explanation of the lower rate of response of the group of retirees who retired between 1968 and 1972 is, we believe, that a higher proportion of individuals who retired in these years had health problems severe enough to discourage or prevent their responding to the questionnaire. Much the lowest response rate was displayed by those who retired in the two years 1968 and 1969. With the exception of the unusually low proportions of respondents who retired in 1968–1969 (and in the case of the utility, in 1970–1972) compared to what would have been expected if response rates had been equal for each year, and of the unusually high proportion for the utility company for 1978, the proportions of respondents found in each of the five years of retirement groups—1968–1969, 1970–1972, 1973–1975, 1976–1977, and 1978—are close to what would have been expected.

In the subsequent discussion we label the group of respondents who retired between 1968 and 1972 "Vintage I," while those who retired between 1973 and 1978 are termed "Vintage II." The distribution of the two vintages by age at retirement is quite similar. A slightly higher proportion of Vintage I retired before they reached age 60 (33%), compared to Vintage II (28%). A slightly higher proportion of Vintage II retired at age 62 (23%), compared to Vintage I (19%). Both vintages were quite similar in the length of the respondents' job tenure. Similarly there was little difference in the distribution of the respondents in the two vintages by type of job.

A slightly higher proportion of Vintage I said that their decision to retire was induced in part by a belief that they could afford to. On the other hand, a slightly higher proportion of Vintage II said that they had retired because of job pressures or adverse treatment of older workers. Health reasons were slightly more important in the case of the earlier vintage; a sense that they had worked long enough motivated a slightly higher proportion of the respondents in the more recent vintage. But the most clear-cut conclusion is that, at least insofar as the respondents are typical of the universe from which they were drawn (and insofar as that universe itself may be typical of a larger universe of early retirees from large organizations), there was little change between 1968 and 1978 in the kinds of reasons that respondents gave for their retirement decisions.

Somewhat surprising is the fact that more of the respondents in Vintage I said that among the reasons for their retirement decision was a belief that they could afford to retire. Between the two periods 1968–1972 and 1973–1978 there was a general improvement in Social Security benefits and in company pension plans. Apparently that improvement did not lead respondents in Vintage II to feel that, at least in retrospect, they were more apt to retire because their economic situation made it an attractive alternative to work. It may be that the continued inflation of the 1970s so concerned many older workers by the mid-1970s that many of them discounted to some extent the value of their future Social Security and pension benefits. If this occurred it could explain that, even though the benefits that they could have expected to receive upon retirement were higher in real terms, the present value of the stream of benefits associated with a long retirement would seem to have been lower, and hence fewer of these individuals facing a retirement decision between 1973 and 1978 felt that they could afford to retire.

It is therefore somewhat surprising to observe that there seems to have been only a moderate difference between the two vintages in their anticipations of inflation at the time of their retirement, insofar as they can recall accurately how rapidly they thought prices would increase. A slightly higher proportion of Vintage I indicate that they gave little or no thought to inflation before they retired. About three out of ten of these respondents recall that this was the case, while only about two out of ten of Vintage II say that they gave inflation little thought. On the other hand, as we have already pointed out, only a very small proportion of respondents in either of the two vintages had, as they recall it, realistic anticipations of the actual course of price increases.

Both vintages had very similar expectations about how satisfactory their retirement experience would generally be, and very similar opinions about how well these expectations were met. Although the first vintage had a longer time for untoward developments to occur, only one out of seven respondents of this vintage said that their retirement experience had been less satisfactory than they had anticipated.

The generally optimistic expectations of the first vintage were fulfilled by subsequent experiences, as were those of the second vintage, in three major aspects of their retirement years. These three dimensions are (a) health status, (b) income status, and (c) social life. Respondents were asked whether they felt that their circumstances at the time of the survey with respect to each of these were better or worse than they had anticipated. It is surprising to note that in spite of the inroads of a decade of inflation, respondents in the first vintage were more likely to feel that their expectations about income were not disappointed (see Table 7.1).

A comparison of the two vintages by the kinds of problems they encountered during retirement (Table 7.2) reveals several differences.

Table 7.1 Actual Health, Income, and Social Life Compared with Preretirement Expectations by Vintages I and II (percentage distribution of respondents)

	Health			Income			Social life		
Vintage	Better	Same	Worse	More	Same	Less	Better	Same	Worse
I	56	18	26	33	29	38	48	28	24
II	54	22	24	28	29	43	43	36	21

In both vintages the largest proportion of respondents gave inflation as the major problem they encountered, particularly when respondents were asked to list the three most serious problems they encountered. But an even larger percentage of respondents in Vintage II, who have not been exposed in retirement to inflation for as long as Vintage I, mentioned inflation as a problem. Next to inflation, health problems, both those of the respondent and of the respondent's spouse, were the most commonly encountered problems. Vintage I respondents, who are in general older, are more likely to report health problems.

For the other categories of problems listed in Table 7.2, there is little difference between the percentage of respondents in either vintage who report that they have encountered these problems. Apparently the problems that retirees have encountered over the last 12 years have little to do with how long they have been retired, with the expected exception of health problems. The earlier our respondents retired the more likely they are to have encountered health problems, either their own or those of their spouse.

Table 7.2 Percentage of Respondents in Vintages I and II Who Encountered Selected Problems During Retirement

Problem	Vintage I	Vintage II
Effects of inflation	88	92
Transportation problems	21	21
Problems with own health	42	35
Problems with spouse's health	35	26
Lack of friends and other social contacts	16	18
Not enough to do and feeling useless	13	15

When we examine the age distribution of the two vintages at the time of the survey (Table 7.3), the heavier incidence of health problems for Vintage I is easily understood.

More than six out of ten of the respondents in Vintage I were at least 70 years old at the time of the survey, while only one out of ten was younger than 65. In contrast, almost four out of ten of the Vintage II respondents were younger than 65, and only one in six was at least 70. In the light of these differences in present age, the higher reported incidence of health problems in Vintage I seems rather small.

Respondents in Vintage I were somewhat more likely to have made large adjustments in their life circumstances and affairs in response to economic pressures. Even so, about half the respondents in both vintages report that they did not have to make more than a small response to economic pressure during the year preceding the survey. Many respondents, however, particularly those in Vintage I, indicated in their written comments that, although they had not yet been forced to make any serious adjustment of their life style in response to economic pressures, they anticipated that such adjustments would soon be necessary if inflation continued at the rate that characterized the time of the survey (winter–spring 1980).

There is a striking similarity in the percentage distribution of respondents in the two vintages by amount of work experience during retirement. About one-quarter of each vintage had some work experience during retirement. About one-eighth of the respondents in each vintage were employed either almost all their retirement years or during a good portion of them. From our point of view the important point is that just as high a proportion of Vintage I says that they have been employed either almost every month or most months as is the case with Vintage II. Apparently a continued and long-lasting commitment to work during retirement is found in a small but still significant proportion of early retirees. These respondents secured employment immediately or soon after retirement and continued this employment with little or no interruption during retirement.

Additional data are provided by the answers given by respondents to a series of questions which asked them (a) whether they were employed at the time of the survey or (b) if not employed at the time of the survey, whether they had been employed at any time in the 12 months preceding the survey. One out of ten respondents in Vintage I were employed at the time of the survey, in contrast to one out of seven of the respondents in Vintage II. A

Table 7.3   Age of Vintages I and II at Time of Survey
            (percentage distribution)

	Vintage I	Vintage II
50-54	0	1
55-59	1	10
60-64	8	26
65-69	29	48
70-74	52	15
75 and older	10	0
Total	100	100

sizable proportion of the respondents who were employed year by year did not choose to work every week in the year. When we add to the respondents who were employed at the time of the survey those who were employed at some time during the previous 12 months, we get an approximation of those respondents who can be considered part of the labor force during the year of the survey. About one out of seven of Vintage I, in contrast to about one out of six of Vintage II, were in this category.

Finally, the response of respondents who were employed at some time during their retirement to a question asking how many different jobs they had had throws additional light upon the continuity of employment.

Answers to this question reveal that a large proportion of the respondents who elected to work during their retirement years established stable and long-lasting employment relationships with one or two employers, in the great majority of cases with only one employer. There may be a close connection between this and the fact that almost all our respondents had long and stable careers with a single employer before their formal retirement. Even though they tended to find postretirement employment with very different kinds of employers and in very different kinds of jobs, they seem to have preferred to maintain stable and long-lived relationships with their postretirement employers.

Vintage I respondents were much more likely to work during retirement for social reasons. Two out of five of Vintage I respondents indicated that social reasons (a desire for more contact with people or a liking for work itself) led to their decision to work during retirement, while one out of five of the respondents in Vintage II went back to work just for social reasons. Eight out of ten respondents with work experience in Vintage I indicated that they were employed during retirement at least in part for social reasons. On the other hand, only about one in ten of the respondents in Vintage I went back to work solely for economic reasons, although one out of two indicated that economic reasons were among the reasons for taking up employment during retirement. One out of six respondents in Vintage II worked solely because of economic reasons, while seven out of ten indicated that economic reasons were among the reasons for postretirement work experience.

A somewhat surprising difference between the postretirement work experience of the two vintages involves the kinds of work schedules worked by the two vintages. Among the respondents actually working at the time of the survey, those in Vintage I tended to work longer hours and more weeks per year. This does not seem to be the result of a selective process whereby those respondents with preferences for longer work schedules emerge among those respondents who were working at the time of the survey. The same phenomenon is clear when the pattern of work schedules by vintage of all respondents who have had any work experience during retirement is examined. Although not quite so marked, longer hours per week and larger number of weeks per year, on the average, clearly characterize Vintage I.

It may be that longer work schedules of respondents in Vintage I are associated with the fact that these same respondents were more likely to have worked during retirement because they like working and because they wanted the social contacts associated with work environments.

Even though they tended to work longer workweeks and more weeks per year, respondents in Vintage I were more likely than respondents in Vintage II to find their postretirement work experiences more satisfying than their preretirement jobs, or at least as satisfying. Only one out of ten of the respondents in Vintage I indicated that he was less satisfied with his postretirement job. In contrast, almost three out of ten of the respondents in Vintage II who had work experience during retirement said that they were less satisfied with their jobs than they were with their preretirement work.

Hourly wage rates of respondents in the two vintages who were working at the time of the survey differed in one respect. While similar proportions of both vintages were paid less than $4.00 an hour (about one-half of both vintages), only slightly more than one out of ten respondents in Vintage I received $7.00 an hour or more, while almost two out of ten of the respondents in Vintage II were paid at least $7.00 an hour in their postretirement jobs.

Even though a smaller proportion of respondents in Vintage I who had work experience said that economic reasons had induced them to work, the economic situation of respondents in Vintage I was in several respects inferior to that of the respondents in Vintage II. Vintage I respondents tended to report lower family incomes during the year before the survey, and they tended to receive monthly total benefits (Social Security benefits plus company benefits) that were lower than respondents in Vintage II. While one out of six respondents in Vintage II received $20,000 or more in family income in the 12 months preceding the survey and only four out of ten said that their family income was less than $10,000, only one out of sixteen in Vintage I received as much as $20,000 as family income, and slightly more than one-half of them received $10,000 or less.

Respondents were asked what work schedule they would prefer if they were to go back to work in the future. Those respondents who did not answer this question can be taken to be those who would be unlikely to work in future under any conditions. Those who did answer can be considered to be those who might, at some time and under some set of conditions, decide to seek employment. A clear-cut difference is evident between Vintage I and Vintage II. In the former, 37 percent would consider work (i.e., answered the future work schedule question), and 63 percent would not consider work (i.e., did not answer). In Vintage II, 59 percent would consider work (answered the question), and 41 percent would not consider work (did not answer).

The pattern of differences in the responses of the two vintages seems to be plausible for other reasons as well. First, it is probable that more members of the older vintage felt that health limitations would stand in the way of work in the future. From the written comments of the respondents, however, there is an even more likely explanation for the higher proportion of respondents in Vintage II who might consider work in the future. Not only were they more concerned about the immediate impact of inflation upon their retirement expectations, but their concern about the impact of inflation on their future life style was much more intense because they anticipated a longer period of deteriorating real income and shrinking real assets.

Another source of the difference is quite possibly that some of Vintage II, who had always anticipated they would reenter the labor market, had not yet made the decision to act because they had been retired only a relatively short time, while members of Vintage I who intended to take up work during retirement had already had ample time to take positive steps. To the extent that a considerable number of early retirees make their decision to retire early, intending to stay out of the labor market for several years but also intending to work in the future whenever economic and/or social reasons become sufficiently strong, it is understandable that Vintage II had not yet reached a point in time when the great majority of those who would ever be likely to work during retirement had already had some work experience.

On the other hand, the fact that more than a third of Vintage I were willing to consider a possible working schedule in the future may indicate that even nonworking retired individuals might still reconsider their decision not to work if pressures such as inflation continued to build and if attitudes continued to shift in favor of moderate levels of work activity by older persons.

At the same time, it should be borne in mind that the nonworking respondents indicated a preference for much shorter hours per week and fewer weeks per year than did those who were working at the time of the survey. Their reentry into the labor market depends therefore not only upon whether certain pressures, such as inflation, continue to build, but also to a large extent upon whether the local labor market can offer older workers the kinds of abbreviated workweek and work year that they prefer.

Although about the same proportion in both vintages had some work experience during retirement at the time of the survey (Vintage I, 23 percent; Vintage II, 24 percent), some, perhaps even a considerable number, of Vintage II who have not yet worked during retirement can be expected to gain some work experience during the next five years, at the end of which they will have been retired on the average as long as members of Vintage I have now been retired. It might therefore be inferred that the rate of postretirement work experience of nonsupervisory personnel may be moving upward.

Another straw in the wind may be the fact that a somewhat higher proportion of the younger vintage say that the reason they have not worked during retirement is because it does not pay. Their written comments indicate that many of them believe that an important reason that postretirement work does not pay is the earnings limitation on Social Security benefits. A drastic reduction of these penalties or their outright abolition might induce some respondents to reconsider their present decision not to seek work.

Mandatory Retirement Compared with Voluntary Retirement

The panel was drawn by the three companies so that 20 percent of the panel were considered by their companies to have been retired because they had reached mandatory retirement age.

The mean age at retirement of respondents who reported that they were mandatorily retired was considerably above the mean of all respondents, 64 compared to 60.6. (Mandatory retirement age for one of the companies was under 65 for part of the period 1968–1978.) The mean age of all respondents at the time of the survey was 67, while the mean age of the mandatorily retired at the time of the survey was 72. The responses about work and other aspects of the retirement experience given by the mandatorily retired come from a group that was on the average 72 years old. The fact that in many respects the retirement experiences of the mandatorily retired is quite similar to that of the respondents as a whole, despite their different reasons for retirement and the discrepancies in their ages, is somewhat surprising. They report about as much work experience during retirement as those respondents who took voluntary early retirement. It should be kept in mind, though, that many of the early retirees retired because of health problems that made retirement necessary rather than optional.

Even more striking is the fact that the present work status of the mandatorily retired does not differ to any significant degree from that of the other retirees. Almost one out of six reported that he or she was either working at the time of the survey or had worked during the past 12 months.

The explanation for the surprisingly high rates of work experience during retirement of this relatively older group of retirees is that many of them not only did not want to retire but also had planned to find work after their mandatory retirement. The proportion of the mandatorily retired who made such plans was 16 percent, much higher than that of other retirees except for those who said that they had retired because of pressures of work or adverse treatment of older workers.

The mandatorily retired were less likely to report that they had encountered health problems during their retirement, but again this is not surprising, even considering the fact that they were on balance several years older than the other retirees. While one-quarter of the respondents who had no work experience during retirement reported that health was one of the reasons for not working, only one out of six respondents who were mandatorily retired reported that health problems were a reason for not working during retirement. On the other hand, one-sixth of the mandatorily retired who had no work experience reported that they could not find suitable job opportunities, a far higher proportion than in the case of respondents who were not subject to mandatory retirement and had no work experience. In fact, if those mandatorily retired who said that they had not worked during retirement because no jobs were available would in fact have worked if suitable jobs had been available, their rate of work experience would have been far higher than that of the rest of the respondents.

In line with this observation is the fact that the mandatorily retired were much more likely to indicate that a change in company or national policy with respect to retirement would have induced them to retire at an older age. Two out of five reported that they would have retired later if mandatory retirement age had been 70 instead of 65. Even though they retired for the most part at age 65, the mandatorily retired did not have as favorable expectations about retirement. Where two-thirds of the panel as a whole reported that they expected that retirement would be very pleasant, even though many of the younger retirees had serious health problems which colored their expectations negatively, only slightly more than half the mandatorily retired looked forward to a very pleasant retirement, and one out of ten thought that it would be unpleasant.

Almost none of the retirees who said that they had retired either because they could afford to retire or because they had worked long enough said that they expected that retirement would be unpleasant. Happily, we can report that the mandatorily retired were more apt than the other respondents to have more satisfactory experiences than they had expected. Only one out of ten said that retirement experiences were worse than expected, compared to one out of seven of the respondents taken as a whole who reported that the retirement experience had been disappointing.

Age at Retirement

The respondents were grouped into six groups by age at retirement. The three companies differ considerably in the age distribution of their respondents at retirement (see Table 7.4). These differences undoubtedly reflect the level and certainty of retirement

Table 7.4   Age at Retirement (by company)

Age group	Utility		Manufact- uring		Chain Store		All respondents	
50-54	9		4		3		5	
55-59	31	48	13	39	25	45	24	44
60-61	8		22		17		15	
62	21		31		18		22	
63-64	14		12		13		13	
		31		30		37		33
65	17		18		24		20	
Total	100		100		100		100	

benefits at different ages by company. The three companies, as we have noted previously, had different retirement benefit plans. The levels of retirement benefits (including the expectation that retirement benefits might be partially increased to reflect price increases) also differed to a considerable extent. Chain Store had set up a stock-sharing plan which, at its inception, seemed to indicate that the retirement incomes its employees would receive would compare quite favorably with those of other large companies in the United States. The behavior of the stock market over the previous decade, however, lowered the real value of the assets that had been accumulated by Chain Store employees for their retirement years. The fact that a higher proportion of the Chain Store respondents retired at age 63 or older seems to be a reasonable response to this change in the expected asset value of their stock accumulations. Another factor that helps to explain the fact that the age distribution of Chain Store respondents has larger proportions retiring in the age groups 63–64 and 65 is the relatively shorter job tenure of the average Chain Store respondent, in particular in the case of women, as pointed out in Chapter 6.

The relationship between age at retirement and year of retirement is of particular interest. Has there been any persistent and noticeable change in this distribution that might throw some light upon the phenomenon of early retirement? To examine this question, we have used five vintages in place of the two vintages used in the first section of this chapter. The five vintages are as follows: Vintage A, year of retirement 1968 or 1969; Vintage B, 1970–1972; Vintage C, 1973–1975; Vintage D, 1976–1977; and Vintage E, 1978.

Table 7.5 Age at Retirement by Five Vintages of Year of
Retirement, Grouped

	Year of Retirement Grouped									
	Vintage A 1968-69		Vintage B 1970-72		Vintage C 1973-75		Vintage D 1976-77		Vintage E 1978	
50-54	3		6		6		5		8	
55-59	33	50	25	46	19	41	24	42	28	52
60-61	14		15		16		13		16	
62	26		17		22		26		21	
63-64	10		15		14		11		13	
65	14	24	22	37	22	36	21	32	14	27
Total	100		100		100		100		100	

The pattern of changes in age at retirement by year of retirement that emerges from Table 7.5 is interesting. A higher proportion of the respondents in Vintages A and E, some 50 percent, reported that they were 61 or younger at the time of their retirement.
At the opposite extreme of the age groups, higher proportions of
Vintages B and C (who retired in the years 1970 to 1975) reported
that they retired at age 63 or older.

Nevertheless, no persistent and sizable changes in the age distribution at retirement are evident from this cross-tabulation of age at
retirement by year of retirement. This is not to say that there might
not have been clear and strong trends evinced by specific subgroups of respondents. It may reflect, indeed, the fact that the very
heterogeneity of the sample and the shifting composition and size
of the subgroups that made up the total group of respondents are
sufficiently large and dynamic as to preclude any strong trend
emerging from the kind of summary cross-tabulation that Table
7.5 presents. The total labor force of the United States is more heterogeneous than is the sample and has probably undergone just as
striking transformations as has the subuniverse represented by the
three companies that were the sources of our respondents. Clear-
cut trends might therefore be even less likely to emerge within the
U.S. population as a whole.

We have paid particular attention to the question of age at retirement in relationship to year of retirement because of the concern
in recent years about declining labor force participation rates of
older age groups. There is no clear-cut evidence from our re-

Table 7.6 Reasons for Retirement by Selected Age Group
(percentage of respondents in each age group
giving indicated reason)

			Age Groups			
Reason	50-54	55-59	60-61	62	63-64	65+
Could afford to retire	16	40	37	41	43	15
Health reasons	64	37	36	26	29	7
Pressure of job or treatment	25	38	35	39	35	7
Mandatory	2	4	4	8	9	96
Disability benefits	39	14	19	10	11	4
Had worked long enough	11	30	43	51	43	11

Note: Columns add up to more than 100 percent because
respondents could, and often did, give more than one
reason for retirement.

spondents of a strong and persistent trend to earlier age at retirement, or to the reverse. If anything, Table 7.5 can be read to indicate the possibility that nonsupervisory employees of large national corporations were tending to retire at somewhat older ages during the mid-1970s.

The age groups differ to a considerable extent in the distribution of the reasons they give for retiring (see Table 7.6). Two age groups stand out from the others. The first is age group 50–54, two-thirds of whom said their health status either made it necessary or desirable for them to retire. The fact that these respondents did indeed experience very real health problems is confirmed by the almost two out of five in this age group who also said that they were retiring in part because they would receive disability benefits from Social Security or from their company benefit plans.

It is also suggestive that few of these respondents stated that they had decided to retire because they could afford to. For some of those who would receive disability benefits, it might have appeared reasonable to report that they could afford to retire. Relatively few of the respondents in this age group said that pressure of work or treatment of older workers were among the reasons they retired. And perhaps of greatest significance, only one out of ten said that he had decided to retire because he had worked long enough.

At the opposite end of the age spectrum, the respondents who were in the age group 65 and over (only a handful were over 65 when they retired) also tended, even more markedly than age group 50–54, to give a single reason for retirement: that they had to retire because of their companies' mandatory retirement policies. A relatively small proportion of this age group also gave other reasons for retirement. One out of six said that in addition to retiring because of mandatory retirement policies, retirement was chosen because it could be afforded. This does not mean that other respondents in this age group did not feel they could afford to retire. But it *can* be taken to mean that being able to afford retirement does not seem to have acted as a positive motive to accept retirement at age 65 for most of this age group. Very few of the respondents in this age group noted that health reasons, pressures of work, or treatment of older workers in their company contributed to their retirement. Moreover, only one out of ten of this age group said that having worked long enough was the reason for retirement. It can be inferred, therefore, although with caution, that many, if not the majority, of the respondents who were retired because of their companies' mandatory retirement provisions would have continued to work at least a year or two longer had they not been forced to retire.

A comparison of the four age groups between ages 55 and 64 illustrates little striking difference in the distribution and frequency of reasons for retirement among the four groups, although the two older age groups were eligible for Social Security benefits. Examined in detail, however, some differences do emerge. Age groups 55–59, 62, and 63–64 were slightly more likely to say, among their reasons for retirement, that they could afford to retire. It is somewhat surprising that two out of five of the retirees who were between 55 and 59 at the time of their retirement felt that being able to afford to retire contributed to their decision. Both this age group and the age group 60–61 were more apt to say that health reasons contributed to their retirement decision, more than one-third of both groups citing health as a reason. Yet, only one out of seven of the respondents in age group 55–59 gave receipt of disability benefits as a reason for retirement, and only a moderately higher proportion, one out of five, of age group 60–61 gave this reason.

More than a third of these age groups said that pressures of work or adverse treatment of older workers were factors that contributed to their retirement decision. A somewhat smaller proportion of age group 55–59, three out of ten, said that they had worked long enough, compared with four or more out of ten for the other three age groups between age 62 and 64. More than one-half the respondents who retired at age 62 said that it was in part because they had worked enough.

Apparently, eligibility for Social Security benefits at age 62 triggered retirement decisions of workers who had also come to the conclusion that they had worked long enough. Knowing that many of their fellow workers had also retired at age 62 and having put in long years with the same company, often at much the same level of skill and responsibility and with little prospect of promotion or job change, a majority of those who retired at age 62 seem to have decided that they had worked long enough. Although only two out of five said they made their decision to retire because they could afford to retire at that age, almost two out of five said that pressure of work or adverse treatment of older workers contributed to their decision to retire.

Postretirement work experience of the different age groups varied widely (Table 7.7). Respondents who were in the two youngest age groups at the time of their retirement (50–54 and 55–59) were more likely to have worked most of the time during their retirement and to be employed at the time of the survey. It will be recalled that about two-thirds of the youngest age group, 50–54, gave health reasons for retirement (and two out of five received disability benefits). Nevertheless, this age group is also most apt to feel that their retirement experience is unsatisfactory, that they are under economic pressure, and that their income is lower than they had expected it to be when they retired.

A relatively high proportion of respondents in this age group whose health permitted were therefore working at the time of the survey and had worked most of the time since retirement. Respondents from the younger age groups (50–54 and 55–59) who have had postretirement work experience are much more likely to have worked full weeks and/or full years. They are also more likely to say that economic reasons were among the reasons for this work experience; but about a fifth of them, only a slightly lower proportion than in the case of older age groups, reported that they worked during retirement for social reasons alone. Moreover, a much higher proportion of the youngest age groups indicated that they might consider work in the future, even though this same age group was much less likely to say that they received as much or

Table 7.7 Work Experience and Work Status at Time of Survey by Age Group at Retirement

Age group at retirement	Work experience during retirement				Work status at time of survey			
	Almost every month	Most months	Not many months	None	Employed	Not at present but in last 12 months	Not in last 12 months but in retirement	None
50-54	14	2	9	75	16	0	9	75
55-59	13	5	11	73	19	2	5	74
60-61	6	5	9	80	13	3	5	79
62	4	5	13	78	9	5	8	79
63-64	8	2	14	77	9	5	9	77
65 and older	4	7	12	77	11	5	7	77

Table 7.8 Work Experience and Employment Status at Time of Survey by Age Group at Time of Survey

| Age group at time of survey | Work experience during retirement | | | | Employment status at time of survey | | |
	Almost every month	Most months	Not many months	None	Employed	Not at present but in last 12 months	Not in last 12 months but in retirement	None
55-59	11	2	11	76	17	2	6	76
60-64	12	4	8	77	17	1	3	78
65-69	7	5	12	76	12	6	6	76
70-74	6	7	13	75	13	4	9	75
75 and older	0	0	8	92	0	3	8	92

more satisfaction from work during retirement as they did from their preretirement job.

Analysis of patterns of time spent in nonpaid activities by age groups reveals very little difference between the age groups. If anything, the youngest age groups are slightly less active, but again it will be recalled that this age group reported much higher levels of health problems both before and after retirement.

Age at the Time of the Survey

Although we have had occasion to remark upon the fact that many of the respondents who had any work experience during their retirement worked a good part of their retirement years, the work experience and present work status of the respondents by their present age (Table 7.8) provides another indication of the extent to which continuity of work experience extends to the upper age groups, with the exception of the age group which was 75 or older at the time of the survey.

Combining those respondents who report that they have worked almost every month with those who say that they have worked most months during their retirement, there is no marked difference between the proportions of the four youngest age groups. With the exception of age group 60–64 (in which one out of six has such work experience) about one out of eight respondents was employed either almost every month or most months. A similar result emerges if we combine those respondents who were employed at the time of the survey with those who, although not employed then, reported work experience during the 12 months preceding the survey. Just under one-fifth of the respondents in all the age groups except the oldest reported either present work or work during the previous 12 months. Since the older respondents tend to prefer (and to work) shorter workweeks and shorter work years, the fact that a higher proportion of those 65 to 74 reported that they were not employed at the time of the survey but that they had been employed at some time during the past 12 months is to be expected.

Differences among the different age groups of respondents at the time of the survey are evident when reasons for work experience in retirement are examined. With age, a marked decrease in the frequency of economic reasons for working is evident, as well as a marked increase in the frequency of social reasons. We have already observed that those respondents who retired relatively early are apt to report that they have health problems, that they face economic pressures, and that they have been disappointed about their income. Moreover, they are generally less satisfied with work during retirement than are respondents who retired later in their lives. The older retirees are, the more apt they are to be working because they like work or like the social contacts available in the workplace, rather than because they are motivated solely or largely by economic pressures.

In the responses of the differing age groups there is no evidence of any significant decline with increasing age in time spent in the five types of nonpaid activities about which we asked the respondents to provide information. In fact, the small group of respondents who were 75 and older at the time of the survey seem if anything to display comparatively high levels of time spent in all activities except paid employment.

CHAPTER 8

The Retirement of Male Nonsupervisory Personnel Compared with Managerial, Professional, and Technical Personnel

Introduction

The structure of the investigation of the retirement experience of nonsupervisory personnel was designed to be as similar as possible to that of the earlier investigation of the experience of managerial, technical, and professional personnel of the same three companies. The latter survey was limited to individuals who held such positions at the time of their retirement and who were earning between $20,000 and $50,000 (in 1978 dollars).

One contrast between the findings of the two studies is of critical importance and determines the presentation of the findings of the second investigation in comparison to the first. We asked the respondents of the earlier study to indicate their sex. Only one woman was among the respondents of one company. In the other two companies, only about one out of twenty respondents was a woman. Although we did discuss the experiences of the women respondents in some detail in the book dealing with the first study, their numbers were so few that we do not feel that their experiences can be contrasted with the much larger proportion of women who made up the second investigation. Few overall statistics, in our view, can as vividly emphasize the extent to which women, in this case women who held long-term year-round jobs, were confined to a limited range of nonsupervisory jobs over a lifetime of work from World War II until the very recent past.

The proportion of women who are now entering the managerial, professional, and technical ranks of large organizations is increasing, although the rate of increase is still only moderate. The significance of the finding from the first survey that only a trivial proportion of women were in the sample, a proportion that was lower than we had anticipated, is that even with the movement of women into these higher occupational levels in the last few decades, few of them have been in these ranks long enough to retire.

Because so few women were in the first survey, we have focused most of this chapter on the contrast between the retirement experience of respondents to the first survey and the retirement experience of the men only in the second survey.

Profile of the Respondents

The mean age at retirement of the managerial, professional, and technical respondents (hereafter termed MPT respondents) was slightly more than 61, while the mean age of the male nonsupervisory respondents (hereafter NS respondents) was just under 61. MPT respondents on the average had worked 35 years for their company before they retired. Male NS respondents usually did not work as many years for their company before retirement, but even in their case the mean number of years was 28.5.

The mean family income before retirement of the MPT respondents was about $40,000 in 1979 dollars. The mean annual salary of the MPT respondents, again in 1979 dollars, was about $32,000, the difference between mean total annual family income and mean annual salary being composed of a mixture of spouse's earned income and income from assets. The mean total annual family income of the male NS respondents was about $23,500 in 1979 dollars. The estimated mean annual earned income in 1979 dollars of male NS respondents who reported their preretirement hourly wage was almost $19,000, the difference between estimated annual earned income and total annual family income being accounted for largely by the earnings of wives.

After these very general observations about the age and income of the respondents to the two surveys, we turn to three major comparisons: (a) the reasons given for retirement by the two groups of respondents, (b) their postretirement work experience, and (c) their other retirement activities.

The Retirement Decision

The MPT respondents and the male NS respondents who had retired early were asked much the same questions about their retirement decision. Table 8.1 summarizes the responses of the two groups of respondents and reveals significant differences between them. Three out of five of the MPT respondents who were early retirees said that among the reasons for their decision to retire was being able to afford to. Only two out of five of the male NS respondents gave this as a reason for retiring early. On the other hand, the NS respondents were more likely to say that they retired at least in part because of health-related reasons and/or because they had worked long enough (about two out of five). Only a quarter of the MPT respondents gave health concerns as a reason for retirement, and a third felt that they had worked long enough.

MPT respondents were more likely (one out of six) to have received an attractive pension offer that helped to induce them to retire, compared to one out of ten NS respondents. It is impossible to compare directly the MPT respondents with the NS respondents with respect to the role that work pressures or treatment of older workers played in their decision to elect early retirement, but it is safe to say that for both groups these reasons were among the most important.

The fact that MPT respondents were more likely to say that they retired in part because they could afford to but less likely to say that they had worked long enough calls for some comment. One would expect that a respondent who gave the first reasons would be likely to give the second, and this relationship is very much the case with respect to NS respondents: almost two-thirds of the male NS respondents who gave among their reasons for retiring early that they could afford to also said that another reason was they had worked long enough. A far smaller proportion of the MPT respondents who said that they had retired at least in part because they could afford to also said that they had retired because they had worked long enough.

The explanation of this difference between the two groups of retirees may be in part that the MPT early retirees were more likely to be considering postretirement work, such as consulting and self-

Table 8.1   Major Reasons for Retirement: MTP and NS
            Respondents (in percentages)

Reason for retirement	MTP respondents	Male NS respondents
Could afford to	61	43
Health-related reason	25	38
Worked long enough	34	43
Attractive pension offer	17	10
Pressures of work	(13+15+10=38)[a]	31
Treatment	(34+11+15=50)[b]	30
Other reasons	31	35

[a]MTP respondents were asked to indicate whether they had retired because of physical demands of their job (13% of the early retirees checked this reason), stresses of decisions and solving problems (15%), or because it was becoming more difficult to meet performance expectations (10%). Since a respondent might have checked more than one of these possibilities, and often did, we cannot add the percentages to get the percentage of respondents who felt at least one of these three types of pressures.

[b]MTP respondents were asked to indicate whether they (1) had risen as far as they could and therefore no longer found the same challenge and satisfaction (34%), (2) were less and less content to work under supervision (11%), or (3) had retired because of a conflict with superiors (15%). We consider that these are reasons for retirement related to the way the company treated older managerial, professional, and technical personnel, but again a respondent could check more than one reason and the percentages cannot therefore be added together. Moreover, these questions are not closely analogous to the question asked of NS respondents, which dealt directly with the treatment of older workers by management, supervisors, and fellow workers.

employment, as part of their retirement; hence they did not consider themselves to be retiring completely, in the sense that their working lives were at an end. In fact, about one out of ten of the MPT early retirees indicated that they had retired from their company because they had either received an attractive job offer from another employer or felt that they should retire early to establish themselves in consulting work or in some form of self-employment.

When those MPT respondents with postretirement employment possibilities are added to the proportion of the MPT early retirees receiving attractive pension inducements to retire from their employers, it becomes understandable that a high proportion of MPT respondents would say they had retired because they could afford to and that a relatively low proportion would say that they had worked long enough.

That health-related reasons were more frequently given by the male NS respondents may be related to two possible factors: (a) their occupations were more apt to induce health problems, and (b) a health problem of a given degree of severity was more apt to be considered a severe burden or threat by NS respondents because of the nature of their occupations.

Almost identical proportions of the MPT respondents and the male NS respondents, about four out of five, reported that in retrospect their retirement decision came at about the right time. A few felt that it came too late, and only one out of five that they should have postponed their retirement decision. Similarly, the proportions of the MPT respondents and the male NS respondents who knew more than a year in advance when they would retire were similar: in both cases about half the respondents had at least a year's foreknowledge.

A major difference in the nature of planning for retirement between the two groups is evident in their response to a question about their plans to work. About one in seven of the male NS respondents said that he planned to work after retirement. In contrast, one-quarter of the MPT respondents reported taking active steps toward postretirement work as part of their planning for retirement, and another 50 percent indicated that they had thought about postretirement employment but had not taken any active steps toward it before they retired. As we indicated earlier, a large proportion of the MPT respondents looked forward to possible consulting work and self-employment or contemplated these types of work. Only three out of ten took steps about or thought about work as a paid employee of a company.

Both groups of respondents generally looked forward to a pleasant retirement and felt, in retrospect, that their retirement experience had lived up to their expectations. The most serious problems that both groups reported encountering centered around either the effects of inflation or problems related to their own health and/or that of their spouse. It seems evident from their responses to structured questions and from the large number of written comments by both groups that inflation was much the most serious

Table 8.2 Work Experience of Managerial, Professional, and Technical (MPT) Personnel and Male Nonsupervisory (NS) Personnel during Retirement (in percentages)

Respondent	Employed at time of survey or in last 12 months	Not employed at time of survey or last 12 months, but at some time	Total with work experience of some kind during retirement (1+2)
MPT	30	7	37
Male NS	20	8	28

problem of their present retirement experience and also loomed as a problem they considered would become increasingly serious in the future. The effects of past inflation and the anticipation of future inflation undoubtedly affected the postretirement decisions to work of many respondents in both groups. We now turn to that subject.

Postretirement Work Experience

MPT respondents were more likely than male NS respondents to have had some work experience during retirement and to be either at work at the time of the survey or to have worked at some time during the previous 12 months (see Table 8.2).

We have called attention to the fact that a large proportion of the NS respondents who had any work experience during retirement, about one half, reported that they had been employed most of the months of their retirement. MPT respondents with work experience were even more likely to report a high degree of continuity of work experience during retirement: about two out of three said they had work experience of one kind or another during most months of their retirement. The character of their work experience also differed significantly from that of the NS respondents. More than half the MPT respondents who worked during retirement reported that their work experience took the form of consulting work or self-employment. About one out of six of NS respondents reported that he was self-employed; none reported that he was a consultant. About one out of six, however, reported working for private individuals.

It is evident that the MPT respondents had a much wider range of possible types of employment experience to select from. It will be recalled, moreover, that a higher proportion of MPT respondents reported that they had planned to work either as consultants or as self-employed individuals rather than as paid employees. The distribution of work experience during retirement by type of employment closely approximates these preretirement intentions of MPT respondents.

The desire, along with the probability that this desire could be realized, to establish oneself as a consultant or as a self-employed professional or technician clearly acted as an incentive on the part of a significant proportion of the MPT respondents to retire early.

A conviction that it was necessary to retire before age 65 to establish oneself in this way was expressed by a number of MPT respondents in their comments and was also indicated in their responses to structured questions. Only a very few MPT respondents indicated that they had worked as consultants or as self-employed individuals because they could find no other employment. The great majority indicated that the reasons for becoming consultants or self-employed during retirement were: (a) they had always wanted to do this kind of work, (b) it provided a possibility of working as long into the future as they wished, (c) it gave them flexibility that they could not secure in working for an employer as a salaried employee. Again, these data and the reasons for choosing to work as a consultant or a self-employed individual agree with the responses of three out of five of the MPT respondents who indicated that being able to afford to retire was among their reasons for early retirement.

Several other reasons given by MPT respondents for retirement, (a) that they had risen as far as they could and no longer felt that their job presented a challenge, (b) that they resented working under a superior, and (c) that there was a conflict between them and a superior, all point to the conclusion that there is a fairly large body of middle-level managerial, professional, and technical personnel who feel that their careers are blocked or are no longer satisfying because of conflict situations. Some of these individuals, after accumulating considerable retirement benefits and other assets, opt to retire from the company that has employed them for most of their adult life in order to take advantage of a wide range of work experiences, particularly as consultants or self-employed individuals, that open to them after they retire.

Like the male NS respondents who were slightly more apt to indicate that they had worked during retirement because of social rather than economic reasons, although half of them indicated that both social and economic reasons were involved in postretirement work decisions, a majority of MPT respondents indicated that they had worked during retirement because they enjoyed the social contacts available from work experience or enjoyed working itself. In addition, one out of five MPT respondents said that he had worked during retirement because it would be good for his physical or mental health, or both.

The great majority of both the MPT and the NS respondents who had work experience during retirement reported that they found their postretirement jobs after a short job search—if not immediately, then within a month or two. The great majority of both groups also reported that their occupations during retirement were quite different from their preretirement jobs, but this did not prevent them from generally feeling at least as much satisfaction in their postretirement work experience as in their preretirement jobs.

It will be recalled that postretirement hourly wage rates and fringe benefits for NS respondents were generally much lower than what they had received in their preretirement jobs. Since the MPT respondents were salaried workers before retirement and then tended to be either consultants or self-employed if they worked during retirement, it was not possible in their case to compare hourly preretirement earnings with postretirement hourly earnings. But we did ask them to indicate what kind of work they performed during retirement. From their answers it is clear that a considerable proportion of the MPT respondents engaged, almost always voluntarily, in occupations that must have been much lower paid than their preretirement work and that had much less status, power, or prestige.

In fact, many of them indicated that one of the satisfactions of postretirement work was that it permitted them to engage in physical work or to make idiosyncratic choices of jobs which, although less well-rewarded in money terms and prestige, gave them great psychic satisfaction, flexibility, and independence.

Male NS respondents were less apt to call attention to the fact that their postretirement work provided great satisfaction because it permitted them to engage in activities that they had long desired to undertake. Nor were they likely to call attention to the fact that their postretirement jobs were radically different from the kinds of work they performed before they retired. Even less were they apt to claim that their postretirement work had given them a new lease on life because it either permitted them to tap long-unused abilities and inclinations or to engage in strenuous outdoor activity. Even though many of the male NS respondents went back to work after retirement because they liked their work or because they enjoyed the companionship which work provided, they still seemed to have a quite instrumental view of the actual work they performed. Not many of them worked after retirement because they felt that they were at last able to engage in the kind of work which provided a high degree of intrinsic satisfaction.

Nonwork Activities During Retirement

One of the major focal points of both investigations of retirement experiences was the nature and extent of nonwork activities in relation to work experiences. Two series of questions dealt with a broad range of nonwork activity. The first set dealt with time spent in various broad categories of effort, including work itself, in a typical week at the time of the survey. The second set asked respondents to compare the frequency of a number of recreational activities, ranging from quite active physical activities to more-or-less passive activities, such as watching television, during the year before retirement, with their frequency during the year before the survey.

Several general observations are in order at the outset of the discussion of nonwork activities during retirement of MPT personnel compared with NS personnel. The first is that there seems to be little systematic relationship between the intensity and duration of work experience during retirement and the amount of time devoted to other major activities or recreational activities. High levels of activity or frequency in one area of activity seem to be associated with generally high levels in many of the other areas.

Second, although there is a good deal of variation among both MPT and NS respondents in specific patterns of activity and in the level of time intensity or frequency, only a small fraction of respondents, less than one in ten, reports generally very low levels of activity. This group of inactive and relatively passive respondents, whether MPT or NS, seems to be largely composed of individuals who have serious, perceived health problems. A small proportion of them also seem to be individuals who became both very depressed by their retirement experience and generally dissatisfied with their general circumstances. Some of them, in written comments, ascribed their low level of nonwork activity to a sense of "uselessness" and "loneliness," often the result of the loss of a spouse or some other close relationship.

Table 8.3 Percentage Distribution of MPT Respondents and
Male NS Respondents by Amount of Time Spent per
Week in Major Activity Areas

Hours spent per week	Male NS respondents	All MPT respondents
Voluntary service		
None	64	43
1 to 10	32	35
10 or more	4	22
Hobbies and recreation		
None	25	8
1 to 10	44	33
10 or more	31	59
Domestic chores		
None	21	8
1 to 10	57	63
10 or more	22	29
Home maintenance work		
None	20	14
1 to 10	60	59
10 or more	20	27

Note: Each grouping totals 100 percent.

The data provided by the MPT and male NS respondents on the
amount of time they were spending in a typical week before the
survey is presented in Table 8.3. Most surveys of time spent in voluntary service have indicated that members of the middle class
tend to spend more time in voluntary service activities than do
members of the working class. Although a large proportion of male
NS respondents would undoubtedly classify themselves as members of the middle class, their educational, income, and occupational status was on the average significantly below that of the MPT
respondents. The time the male NS respondents reported spending in voluntary service differed in several respects from that reported by MPT respondents. Almost two-thirds of them spent no
time in such activities, while only two out of five MPT respondents
spent no time. More than a fifth of the MPT respondents reported
spending more than 10 hours a week in voluntary service, while
only one out of twenty-five male NS respondents spent that much
time.

The pattern of time spent in hobbies and recreational activities is more similar, but here again MPT respondents report spending more time, on the average. A quarter of the male NS respondents report spending no time at all on hobbies and recreation in contrast to one in twelve of the MPT respondents. And of those respondents in both groups who reported spending time on these activities, only three out of ten of the male NS respondents reported spending more than 10 hours a week, while six out of ten MPT respondents, double that proportion, reported that much time spent on hobbies and recreational activities.

Except for the fact that a higher proportion of male NS respondents, one out of five, reported spending no time in domestic chores, the pattern of time spent both on domestic chores and on home maintenance reported by MPT respondents differs little from that reported by male NS respondents.

MPT respondents were asked to answer somewhat more detailed questions dealing with recreational and other activities, but in general the differences in time spent in major activities that is revealed by Table 8.3 is reflected by differences between MPT respondents and male NS respondents in the frequency with which they engaged in specific recreational activities. Most striking is the difference in how often the two groups of respondents engaged in active sports in the year before the survey. Less than one in five of the NS respondents reported frequent involvement in active sports, whereas two out of five of the MPT reported this level of participation in active sports. A large proportion of both groups reported that they frequently were engaged in gardening, but here again the MPT respondents were more likely to participate. Another popular recreational activity in retirement, travel, was engaged in by large proportions of both groups, a fourth of the NS respondents and more than a third of the MPT respondents.

The conclusion that emerges from this comparison of the frequency with which MPT respondents and male NS respondents engaged in recreational activities is that the more physically demanding the activity, the less likely were male NS respondents to report engaging in it as often as MPT respondents. Where the activity was physically undemanding, like watching television, both groups report about the same frequency of involvement.

CHAPTER 9
Retirement: Change and Continuity

Introduction

The recent increase in the numbers of men and women who have elected to withdraw from the labor force before reaching age 65, still the official norm for retirement in our Social Security legislation, is part of the larger problem of how people are changing allocation of time between such things as education, market work, nonmarket productive activity, and leisure over their lifetime. These general problems are in turn embedded in even larger social problems arising from long swings in such demographic factors as birthrates and deathrates, as well as those relatively abrupt shifts in demography associated with factors such as war, immigration (legal and illegal), shifts in values, particularly those associated with work and leisure, and changing conceptions of the future.

There is another way, however, of looking at one set of problems associated with early retirement. From this different perspective, early retirement is viewed as a source of problems encountered by societal institutions at the same time as early retirement itself is in part the result of the policies (or non-policies) and the actions (as well as the inactions) of these institutions. In other words, early retirement causes problems for some of those who choose to retire early, and it in turn results from problems individuals have encountered in their interactions with employing institutions and with the government.

Only a few years ago early retirement was viewed as a solution to problems encountered by individual workers and their employers. Indeed, the creation of the Social Security system and the progressive lowering of the age of eligibility for benefits was considered an important element in a general labor market strategy designed to reduce the size of the labor force in the face of inadequate number of jobs. In this strategy older workers were to be induced to step aside in favor of younger workers.

From a different but related standpoint, employers also favored policies that would induce older workers to retire. Both strategies could initially be purchased on the cheap: the first, because Social Security benefits were never funded, and initially a very large number of workers supported a relatively small number of beneficiaries; the second, because an abundant supply of relatively highly educated younger workers was available, again on the cheap, to move in to replace those older workers who elected early retirement. Moreover, while older men were withdrawing from the labor force, middle-aged women were moving into the labor force in large numbers.

Although gerontologists were accumulating data indicating that older workers were as productive, or almost as productive, as younger workers and had qualities of character and experience which made them particularly valuable to employers, company executives in charge of personnel policies and benefit plans encountered evidence and analysis indicating that older workers were more costly to employ and more difficult to train. Moreover, their very presence was often seen as a kind of "icecap," to use the rather nasty metaphor that was current, that prevented younger workers from moving upward through the ranks of the plant and the company headquarters.

In sum, the tilt of both national and company policies was in the direction of easing older workers out of the labor force at progressively earlier ages. That the impetus to leave the world of work took in part the form of economic incentives, often accompanied by other types of pressures that were neither uniformly felt nor pleasantly perceived by those pressured, does not alter the fact that older workers tended more and more to believe that they should retire as soon as "they could afford to," whatever that vague phrase might come to mean in the context of increasing inflation.

Moreover, the policies of several of the most powerful and prominent unions in the country reinforced national and company policies. Unions whose members worked on assembly lines or under conditions that imposed severe physical or psychic stress upon workers, in some of the largest and most profitable companies in the country, demanded and received pension plans in which eligibility for retirement benefits increasingly took the form of an age-tenure combination. In these industries retirement in one's fifties at what were perceived to be very substantial pension benefits became more frequent. Since these industries were prominent and the provisions of their pension plans with respect to early retirement were widely publicized, many older workers began to assume that the norm for retirement age was not some fixed age such as 65, but was rather flexible and moving downward.

Public pension policies, particularly with respect to several prominent categories of public employees—the military, policemen and firemen, and the like—also often permitted and encouraged retirement at very early ages. All of this took place in an economy which was expanding rapidly and in which productivity seemed to increase steadily and strongly. With little decrease in the length of the average workweek or in the number of weeks worked per year, the American worker seemed to be determined to take at the end of his life whatever increase in lifetime leisure the increase in per capita income permitted. With concomitant increases in longevity and improvements in physical condition, a large pool of older individuals emerged whose worklife was ending in their late 50s or early 60s, although their life span had been increased by several decades.

This, then, is the backdrop against which the story told by our respondents, both in their answers to the structured part of the survey instrument and in their written comments about their experiences and about their opinions and feelings, must be understood. This background should remind the reader that national policies with respect to older workers and retirement and the company policies that evolved over the same period were formed in an economic climate with two major characteristics: (a) a continual concern over the adequacy of jobs in the face of an increasing labor force and hence a tacit support of national and private policies that tended to decrease the number of older workers, and (b) an unprecedented boom in the economy itself in which increases in GNP, in productivity, and in the size of the labor force went hand in hand, and in which it seemed for a time that almost any social policy with widespread support and which seemed to be beneficent could be afforded.

Finally, all this took place at a time when neither Social Security, the public system of old age support, nor the private system of company-funded pensions had reached maturity. The true cost of both systems was not yet appreciated by most public and private

officials, and certainly not by the public. Nor was there a widespread awareness of the effects of early retirement upon the individuals who had elected (or been forced) to retire before age 65.

Many of these individuals found early retirement to be what they
had anticipated, a most welcome surcease from long years of physically and emotionally demanding work. For others, however, early
retirement was not entirely an unmixed blessing. Since it involved a
very heterogeneous population, some inevitably encountered
problems. And some problems emerged in the 1970s that few, if
any, were able to escape. We turn first to those problems. Without a
due recognition of the kinds and severity of problems encountered
by individuals, policies that affect older workers and early retirement are likely to be both insensitive and faulty in conception.

The Problems of Early Retirement: The Individual

Although a majority of our respondents indicated that they had retired because they had worked long enough and could afford to, a
sizable fraction said that they retired in part because of the pressures of work and the treatment of older workers in their
workplace. Only rarely did they indicate that it was the treatment
of older workers by fellow workers that was a problem; rather it
was the treatment accorded them by supervisors or by what they
felt to be the management of the company. There was considerable
diversity among the three companies in the proportions of respondents who reported these problems. General company policy
undoubtedly plays a significant role in creating a belief that older
workers are under pressure or are not being treated fairly or with
sensitivity.

Most of the respondents who chose to retire early reported that
they knew a considerable time in advance when they would retire.
About a quarter, however, had little or no advance knowledge of
the date of their retirement. It is true that those least likely to know
in advance were those whose health suddenly worsened to an extent that made retirement either necessary or desirable. Almost
half of those who reported that they had less than three months'
advance knowledge also reported that their health status was a reason for retirement. Yet almost a third of those who retired because
of job pressures or the treatment of older workers also reported
that they had less than three months' foreknowledge of the date of
retirement. Although respondents in the first group were relatively
unlikely to work during retirement, respondents in the second
group were relatively likely to work during retirement.

Lack of knowledge of when retirement would take place was also associated with less planning for retirement, with a much higher probability that a respondent felt that retirement had come too soon, with less use of guidance and counseling services, and with less access to sources of information about retirement. Finally, lack of foreknowledge was associated with a much higher probability that a respondent would be dissatisfied with the retirement experience as a whole. To some extent of course this is also a result of the fact that a large proportion of those who had little advance knowledge also had health problems during retirement, and health problems are major determinants of the quality of the retirement experience.

Once actually retired, respondents reported that they encountered a number of problems. Much the most important in their view were inflation and inflation-related problems. Respondents were troubled because company pensions were not fully indexed for inflation and did not keep up with the future pension benefits scheduled for current employees of their companies. Uncertainty over any ad hoc increases in their pension benefits increased both their anxieties and their irritation, which was apt to take the form of resentment against governmental employees, in particular, whose retirement incomes, in their view, were fully indexed.

The illiquidity of much of their assets, particularly their houses, and the increase in the cost of running and maintaining a house, were other aspects of the problem of inflation, as was the fact that the behavior of the stock market had resulted in serious losses for those respondents whose retirement income was linked to accumulations of stock. As one of the respondents remarked, and his comment was typical of many others, "There is no way to keep up with inflation and no way to beat it. You just have to stand there and suffer it and hope that either you or it don't last too much longer!"

Next to inflation, health problems were the most serious. These might be the problems of the respondent or the respondent's spouse, or, as in many instances, of both. The heavy economic burden of rising medical costs preoccupied many respondents, both those with illnesses and those who feared possible illness in the future. Many respondents wrote that one of the most trying aspects of the retirement experience was the fact that their medical bills were no longer covered by the kind of benefit plan they had enjoyed while employees of their companies. These respondents are firmly convinced that company health benefits should be lifelong.

Respondents who reported that they had worked during retirement almost all reported that they had been able to secure jobs after a relatively short search, and most respondents reported that they were either as satisfied or more satisfied with their postretirement work as with their preretirement jobs. Moreover, some respondents wrote that in their opinion there were plentiful job opportunities for retired people.

Problems associated with postretirement work therefore arose not from obtaining employment as such, but from obtaining suitable jobs at suitable pay. To secure postretirement employment many of the respondents had to accept large reductions in hourly pay and in fringe benefits. These reductions were very large when one considers the general reluctance of American workers to accept reductions in pay and job status before they retire.

Although more than half the respondents who worked during retirement reported that they were glad that their skills and experience were appreciated and were happy to be able to do things postretirement which they could not do before they retired, another group of respondents was clearly dissatisfied with their jobs. More significant, a fairly large number of respondents who had no postretirement work experience reported that this was because they could not find suitable jobs and/or it did not pay to work. Since many of these respondents did not report unsuccessful searches for work, the conclusion seems inescapable that many retired people are so convinced that the jobs available to retired people are unsuitable, either because of the pay scales or because of the content of the jobs, that they do not bother to search at all.

Such reports imply that the presently reported rates of postretirement work experience may drastically understate the potential pool of older retired workers who would work if they could find work at pay scales approximating those they enjoyed before retirement, particularly if they could have the option of reduced workweeks and work years and/or flexible work schedules.

It also is significant because it might imply that many of those respondents who did accept work during retirement at hourly pay rates far below their preretirement, relatively high, pay scales somehow had come to alter radically their conception of themselves as workers and their conception of work itself. But the reader will recall how frequently those respondents with postretirement work experience reported that they chose to work during retirement either entirely or in part for social reasons. For many respondents, postretirement work would seem to have social dimensions at least as important as the economic dimensions.

It will be recalled that postretirement work is also related to the problem of the timing of the retirement decision. The great majority of our respondents felt that they retired at the right time. But of those who in retrospect felt that the timing was wrong, almost all felt that they had retired too soon. Moreover, while a third of the respondents said they would have been receptive to company policies designed to delay retirement, only a fifth indicated that they would have been receptive to policies designed to induce earlier retirement.

Among these possible company policies, four were closely linked together.* These were policies designed to offer older workers (a) more flexible schedules and/or shorter hours, (b) better chances for promotion and/or raises, (c) job reassignments that reduced job pressures, and (d) retraining. Retraining, however, in itself would not have induced more than a handful of the respondents to delay retirement. The other three policies appealed to a much larger number of the respondents; if a respondent indicated that one of the three policies might have had an effect upon the timing of his retirement decision, he was quite apt to indicate that the other two would also have had an effect. The policy that appealed to the largest number of respondents was "job reassignment that reduced pressures of work," followed in attractiveness by a change in mandatory retirement age to age 70 from age 65.

Nevertheless, a change in mandatory retirement age alone would not have induced more than one out of ten respondents to delay retirement. We can conclude that a set of interlinked policies is necessary, policies that not only make later retirement possible but also offer positive inducements in the form of either (a) reassignment to jobs perceived as having less pressure associated with them, (b) more flexible and/or shorter work schedules, or (c) promotions and raises, even if these are associated with reassignments. The answers given by our respondents indicate that in addition companies that provide clear and firm guidelines to supervisors and to management that age discrimination will not be tolerated are more likely to create a climate in which older workers will take advantage of other policies to delay their retirement. We also conclude that retirement itself will have to be conceived of as a process taking place over a variable period of time in which a number of adjustments—in hours, job assignments, pay and status—will take place, not mechanically, but in the light of the idiosyncratic character of groups of workers and of individual workers themselves.

*For additional data on responses by sex and company affiliation to possible changes in company policies, see Table 5.3.

The Company and Early Retirement: The Utilization of Older Workers

The discussion of problems associated with early retirement has focused on the individual worker. The company policies discussed have been related to the timing of the retirement decision, again from the point of view of the individual, as if it were a foregone conclusion that companies would desire to initiate such policies.

Most company pension systems take the form of the defined benefit plan that creates strong incentives to hire younger rather than older workers. We want to emphasize that the differentials between the cost of hiring older workers and younger workers is an inescapable feature of the defined benefit pension system. The steeper the gradient of hourly wages is with respect to age, the more the pension benefits are based upon a formula which weights the last years of employment more heavily than earlier years, and the more generous the pension formulas are, the larger these differentials become.*

Not only is the problem of the usual pension system of differential costs by age very serious from the point of view of the utilization of older workers, but also the implications of raising mandatory retirement age to 70 (and quite possibly making any mandatory retirement by age illegal, either through legislative or judicial action, in the near future) have not yet been fully appreciated or acted upon by employing institutions.

Quite simply stated, an open-ended worklife increases the risk to a company associated with the retention or hiring of older workers. This risk also increases with any increase in the obstacles placed in the way of dismissing older workers for cause, or conversely, with any increase in the incentives older workers have for not retiring. Needless to say, rapid inflation provides such an incentive for many older workers.

Prima facie, the dismissal of a worker who has had many years of employment with a firm is apt to be seen as an instance of age discrimination, particularly if there is substantial evidence that losses in productivity due to increasing age are compensated by valuable attributes brought by older workers to the work environment, such as judgment, loyalty, reliability, and so forth. To document a de-

*For a full discussion of this problem, see Burt S. Barnow and Ronald G. Ehrenberg, "The Costs of Defined Benefit Plans and Firm Adjustments." Their paper presents models that illustrate the size of these cost differentials under a wide range of assumptions.

cline in productivity to the satisfaction of the courts endeavoring to enforce the provisions of the Age Discrimination in Employment Act, as amended (and likely to be amended more in the future) is certain to be difficult in most cases, and possibly impossible in many. How, for example, can one document the declining productivity of an individual who is a member of a work crew where only productivity of the crew as a whole can be measured? How can one document a decrease in productivity where output is a service rather than a good?

Moreover, where a company does try to dismiss an older worker for cause and the matter comes to litigation, courts are increasingly apt to ask whether the company has made good faith efforts to help the older worker adjust to age-related physical and mental deficits through the provision of job reassignment, retraining, flexible and shorter work schedules, counseling and guidance, and so forth. It is in this economic and legal setting that companies will have to initiate and develop programs that lead to effective utilization of older workers, while at the same time minimizing the risk or possible abuse of policies designed to protect the older worker from age discrimination.

We believe that a major pillar of any company's policies with respect to older workers and early retirement is a resolute recognition and acceptance of the fact that the productivity of many workers older than what is now the average age for retirement can be perfectly acceptable to the firm. Older workers are unlikely to persist in jobs that overtax their physical capacities. And older workers who have serious and debilitating health problems are the very ones who wish or are forced to retire at relatively early ages by their own physical state. This generalization will become increasingly valid as increasing automation decreases the physical demands placed upon workers, as the average educational achievement of older workers more nearly approaches that of the labor force as a whole, and as various forms of service work in which qualities of experience and character play an essential role increase relative to routine production jobs.

It is clear that a second major pillar is the understanding that older workers have particular needs, as do younger workers, and must be treated in ways that recognize and respect the differences between age groups. For example, conventional forms of retraining programs do not usually appeal to or attract many older workers. Only a relatively small number of our respondents, for example, said that they would have welcomed programs that allowed older workers to be retrained.

This does not mean that older workers do not want to do new things at work. In fact, job reassignment for older workers was one of the possible company policies that particularly appealed to our respondents. Moreover, more than half of the respondents who worked during retirement indicated that the change in the kind of work they did was one of the positive aspects of postretirement work.

But older workers do not like to be forced to do things. They wish to change at their own pace and when they want to make the change. They want to be respected and feel that they have earned and deserve respect. (Some of them were quick to take offense at company policies which they perceive to slight them or to represent subtle pressure to induce them to retire.) At the same time, many of our respondents expressed resentment that retirement meant an abrupt break of all ties to their company; that the company found no value in maintaining other than perfunctory relations with them after employing them for a lifetime.

It would seem that large organizations, at small cost to themselves, could furnish information to their retirees about the affairs of the company. Retired workers often feel that their pensions depend upon the continued existence and prosperity of the company from which they retired. Often they are simply interested in what happens in the workplace, what new products the company is developing, and what new ways of making products are being introduced.

Although it might seem a thankless task to keep retired employees informed, many of them have a deep-seated interest in and loyalty to their company. The reputation of the company and its products and/or services is in part in their hands; but more particularly, the reputation of the company as an employer depends to some extent upon what they impart to their communities. If the employees feel neglected or that their contribution over many years to the company's survival and growth is not appreciated, the message will be directly and indirectly passed to the wider community that the company uses up workers and then casts them aside.

A point that should be emphasized about older workers and their attitudes toward their company is that their good will and appreciation cannot be bought solely by generous pension benefits at retirement and adjustments of these pension benefits to keep up with inflation. If older workers have perceived that working conditions put undue pressure upon them as they grew older, if they feel that their company pursued inflexible policies in the face of the specific needs of older workers, or if they feel that age discrimination has been permitted or encouraged by the company's management, they are likely to carry their resentments into retirement, unabated and, in some cases, heightened with the passage of time.

Older workers, including those who have retired, often possess invaluable skills and experience. Large companies, in particular those whose production processes and products are complex and technologically highly sophisticated or whose organizational structure is based upon subtle and complicated personal interchanges between team members, need many of the qualities of skill, experience, character, and judgment that are embedded in many older employees. This combination of traits, valuable both to the individual and to the company, is what is sometimes referred to as firm-specific human capital. One of the most unfortunate and costly aspects of early retirement is the abrupt loss of this human capital.

One of the advantages of carefully phased retirement expressed in flexible work schedules, shorter hours, job reassignment, and so forth is that it prevents much of this waste of human resources. The responses received in this survey indicate that firm-specific human capital need not be lost during retirement if the former employee's services are made available to the company on an ad hoc and temporary basis, with the clear understanding on both sides that good faith efforts will be made to make the relationship as beneficial as possible to both and that the employee will remain in a formal retirement status.

The company can inform its older workers that it will, whenever possible, recall older workers when temporary need for their skills and experience arises, and then can create a roster of retired employees who have expressed an interest in such an ongoing relationship.

But only a minority of retirees can be expected to want to work after retirement. What of the rest of them? What, according to our respondents, should the company's relationship be to them? In some cases all that a company can do is to keep former employees informed. One of the striking findings of the survey, from our point of view, was the extent to which a postretirement work decision resulted from social needs of the respondents. Although few of them say that a lack of friends or feelings of boredom or uselessness are major problems of retirement, a number of them did indicate in their comments the importance of their preretirement relationships with fellow workers. A maintenance of these social ties, even an expansion of them, could be of great value to many retirees.

One of the problems of older persons, particularly as they move from the status of the young-old to that of the old-old, is the gradual decline in the strength and coherence of the social networks that have given shape and meaning to their existence. One of the objectives of governmental policy, particularly on the national level, has been to bolster and to recreate where possible these social support networks. One of the most important of these networks, particularly for many nonsupervisory workers and especially for many women, who can be expected to need them longer than men, is the network that evolved out of many years of working with the same group of workers.

It is our impression that where the number of retired workers in a community from the same company is sufficiently great, the creation of company centers in which these can continue to meet and carry on a wide range of activities is highly desirable. The cost of such centers is apt to be substantial; and how to create them initially, how to organize them, how to maintain them, and how to involve retired individuals in their activities are all difficult problems. But if, in fact, such centers would be of value to retired employees, then the more they themselves are involved directly in the creation, direction, and maintenance of such centers, the less difficult these problems will be.

Much effort now goes into the creation of social networks among the aging, and to fail to cultivate to the fullest the surviving roots of the social networks between employees of large companies that persist into retirement would be to overlook the obvious. Here, again, is an area where the experiences of companies that have taken the lead (or even failed in the effort) can provide a basis for company efforts.

Older Workers, Early Retirement, and National Policy

At present, the elements of national policy with respect to older workers, early retirement, and the problems of the aging consist of three separate sets of policy and administrative initiatives. The most important and the oldest is the Social Security Administration and its manifold programs. A second set of initiatives is that provided by the Age Discrimination in Employment Act and its amendments. The third set of initiatives and programs is that carried on by the Administration on Aging of the U.S. Department of Health and Human Services.

We have already had occasion to discuss some of the major impacts of Social Security policy upon older workers and early retirement. Many of the proposed changes in the operation of Social Security, which have been the subject of discussion in the last few years and are currently under consideration both by Congress and the Administration, are designed to tilt Social Security in favor of retirement at later ages than is now the case. The object of these changes is to provide a solution to the pressing problem of financing Social Security benefits over the next few years. Serious as that problem is, the policies that are adopted will also have an effect upon the incentives of older workers either to withdraw from the labor force before age 65 or to remain in the labor force after that age. To date the implicit objective of national policy has been to shunt older workers aside. From our sample it is clear that a considerable proportion of those older workers who have retired before age 65 have done so because of acute or chronic illness which renders work either impossible or intolerable. Adequate provision for this subset of older workers, however, does not have to mean unnecessarily large and, from a social viewpoint, unproductive incentives for healthy and vigorous older workers to retire before their time.

We have deliberately used the expression "before their time." We believe that work for the healthy and vigorous provides much more than income, and we believe that many of the respondents, both through their actions and through their comments, have illustrated and bolstered this contention. From their experiences and comments we conclude that they should be encouraged to contribute their energy, talent, skill, and experiences as long as they find it rewarding economically and socially to do so.

An additional dimension exists for one half of the population. The responses of women to our survey highlight the extent to which their worklives have been shadowed by pervasive sex-discrimination. The overwhelming majority of the women respondents were not part-time workers, in and out of the labor market, but with few exceptions they were confined to a limited range of occupations. Their hourly rates of pay were much lower, and hence their Social Security earnings record was systematically and radically lower than was the case for most men. Now they face a longer period of retirement, and most subsist on the basis of relatively low Social Security benefits.

The differentials in earnings of the men and women respondents to our study can only be understood as being largely the consequence of sex-discrimination. This discrimination was not the result of deliberate company policy, but arose from a "natural" policy of assigning and restricting women workers to occupations for which societal wage norms were less than for the men. The education that men and women brought to their jobs was much the same, and both women and men had much the same length of experience on the job (in both cases several decades on the average). Since it is hard to maintain that the men either did more difficult or more necessary work than the women, it is difficult to avoid the conclusion that wage differentials were the result of sex discrimination.

We have raised this issue in the context of the lifelong differentials in earnings of men and women employed by three major corporations. The combination of relatively low earnings during a lifetime of work, of low total benefits from Social Security and company pensions, of a much higher incidence of currently nonmarried status among women, and of much longer life expectancy is sure to place many of these women at much higher economic risk at some time in the future, if not in the present. The great majority of these women either supported themselves or contributed to the support of their families through several decades of full-time work. Many of them now run the risk of becoming dependent upon public agencies or upon their families, or else suffering such severe economic deprivation that both their health and their self-respect are severely damaged.

The Age Discrimination in Employment Act, with its amendments, provides the legal basis for affording protection to older workers who have suffered discrimination because of age. Although not many of our respondents reported that they had encountered age discrimination in searching for postretirement employment, some believe that it is essential that the provisions of ADEA be forcefully applied to protect older individuals. Their numbers are likely to increase in the future. Since they are not likely to have the support of institutions such as labor unions to assist them in gaining the protection of ADEA, they will need general and specific information about ADEA. In particular they will need to have confidence that they can gain access to ADEA promptly and without undue cost.

But not only after retirement must ADEA protection be effectively provided. A significant proportion of the respondents reported that they had retired in part at least because of the treatment of older workers, either by supervisors or by the management of their companies. It should be added that in their employment policies the three corporations who provided the panel are among the most enlightened of large American companies. Even so, it is obvious that many older workers feel that they are subject to pressures that directly or indirectly induce some of them to retire. With the increase in the legal age for mandatory retirement (and the likelihood that within a few years all mandatory retirement by age will be made illegal) it would seem essential that the ADEA be forcefully administered to prevent the emergence of widescale pressures upon some older workers to retire.

In addition, labor market information specifically targeted to older workers might be developed and efficiently delivered to them. Second, training programs targeted on older workers might be initiated. It may be that some of these programs should use a "correspondence school" format. The programs should be built around the interests of older workers and should include training in areas that have traditionally been considered hobbies but which, in many cases, could provide older retired individuals with remunerative and rewarding activities to be pursued at home or in conjunction with other older individuals in their communities.

Finally, a number of federally sponsored programs already provide various kinds of services to older workers. Although much has been done by the various federal agencies responsible for these programs to get information to those who are eligible, we believe that it is desirable that such information programs be coordinated and that an older worker who is contemplating retirement have access to a comprehensive description of what these programs provide and how to gain access to them.

The Social Security Administration is in a position to provide to all covered workers a simple but important piece of information: an annual comprehensive statement of their earnings record, similar to private pension programs, to provide them with an estimate of what their benefits will be if (a) they have no further covered earnings and (b) if their future earnings to specific ages continue at their current level. Such information could be generated automatically at relatively little cost with modern data processing equipment. It would materially assist older workers in planning effectively for retirement and for postretirement work and would be more efficient than the current system, which leaves it to the initiative of individual workers to check upon their earnings record every three years to ensure that it is accurate.

Since many of our respondents indicated that in retrospect they felt they had retired too soon, we believe that any action to improve the information available to older workers as they contemplate retirement would reduce the number of those whose retiring timing proved wrong. This might also have the desirable effect of increasing the number of older workers who elect to continue working rather than to retire.

Suggestions for Additional Research

We would like to take this opportunity to make several suggestions for additional research. Our first suggestion is that the Bureau of Labor Statistics institute, and repeat at stated intervals, a program of specific surveys similar to the programs now in place dealing with youth, women, and several minorities, the results of which are contained in Special Labor Force Reports. This program should be ongoing, national in scope, and focused both on older workers in the years immediately preceding retirement and upon work experience of older workers, in particular upon those who have formally retired. It would be desirable to coordinate such a program of ongoing surveys of older workers with Social Security Administration research and survey programs. This program should be initiated as soon as possible. There is no question that there will be increasing need for more detailed survey data on older age groups.

Research on the relationship between family composition, the retirement decision, postretirement work experience, and other aspects of retirement is also desirable. Such research should focus on five basic types of families: (a) the traditional one-earner husband-wife family; (b) the family composed of husband and wife, both full-time workers before retirement; (c) the divorced and separated; (d) the widowed; and (e) the never married. The rapid changes now taking place in the configuration of the American family have potentially major implications for the length of the worklife and for postretirement economic and social status.

The relationship between chronic and acute health problems and work activity in older workers also requires attention. Where an acute illness might be a passing phase and lead only to a short interruption in the worklife of a younger worker, it could lead to a termination of work for an older worker. Chronic disease processes may similarly lead to retirement, even though adequate treatment of the underlying illness coupled with sufficient flexibility in work schedules and work loads, including job reassignment, might have led to many more years of economically useful work and improved physical well-being. Many of our respondents who retired in part because of health-related reasons reported that they worked during retirement.

Research focusing on health, preretirement work activity, the retirement decision itself, and postretirement work activity would help to establish some of the complex causal relationships between health status and work activity, and might reveal specific circumstances where continued work activity, even if at a reduced level, has been associated with the amelioration of health problems of older workers.

Our final suggestion for research focuses on what, in our view, may become a pressing national concern in the years to come. It also stems from a central finding in our investigation. Retirees who had returned to work after retirement reported a very brief job search of usually less than one month's duration. Three in four of these work returners, however, earned *less than one half of their preretirement wage rates and an even larger number received either nominal fringe benefits or none at all*. The willingness to work at such low wages after a lifetime of work for much higher wages and fringe benefits raises a number of questions about the reasons for this drastic lowering of the "reservation wage."

• Do older workers believe that age discrimination automatically excludes them from "good jobs," and in failing to apply for these, do they create a self-fulfilling situation?

• By doing so, do they unwittingly create a stereotype of the older worker as a marginal worker, subject to the usual types of institutionalized discrimination; and do they send signals not only to employers, but to other older workers who might be interested in returning to work, but not at such low wages?

• Since social reasons for returning to work received so much emphasis in our surveys, and since so many reported receiving as much, if not more, satisfaction from postretirement as compared to preretirement work, did psychic income swamp consideration of money income?

• How adequate was the labor market information on which these work returners acted? Did the briefness of the job search indicate that having a "sure thing" was a primary motivation?

• Did the cost and inconvenience of the "journey to work" act as a barrier to getting work in the primary sector?

These and related questions might properly be made the subject of further research with a particular emphasis upon the perceptions older workers have of their opportunities in the job market.

APPENDIX A
Retirement Activities Study Questionnaire

I. WE WOULD LIKE TO BEGIN WITH SOME QUESTIONS ABOUT YOUR RETIREMENT DECISION.

1. I retired from "Utility" ( ).
   "Manufacturing" ( ).   I retired in _____.
   "Chain Store" ( ).   year

2. I was _____ years old when I retired and I had worked _____ years for this company.

3. In the year before I retired, my job with this company was

   _____
   (give Job Title or brief description of what you did)

4. I retired because (check all boxes that apply to you)

   a) I could afford to retire ( ).
   b) My health made it necessary ( ) or desirable ( ) to retire.
   c) The pressures of work were getting too great ( ).
   d) I did not like the way older workers were being treated by management ( ), supervisors ( ), by other employees ( ).
   e) It didn't pay to keep working ( ).
   f) I had reached mandatory retirement age ( ).
   g) I had worked long enough ( ).
   h) My company offered me a special pension arrangement that made it attractive to retire when I did ( ).
   i) My health qualified me for Social Security disability benefits ( ), and/or benefits from my company's benefit plan ( ).
   j) My supervisors suggested that I retire before I had reached age 65 ( ).
   k) There was a reduction of employment in my part of the company and I was laid off so I retired at that time ( ).
   l) Other _____

   _____
   (please describe briefly)

5. All things considered, I think that I decided to retire:

   a) at about the right time ( ).
   b) too soon ( ).
   c) too late ( ).

(2)

6. I knew about when I was going to retire:

   a) more than three years before I actually retired ( ).
   b) between one and three years before I retired ( ).
   c) less than a year but more than three months before I retired ( ).
   d) less than three months, but it did not come as a surprise ( ).
   e) I did not know in advance ( ).

7. Among the things I planned for in thinking about retirement were:
   (check all that apply)

   a) where I would live after retirement ( ).
   b) to move to a different community ( ).
   c) how to spend most of my time ( ).
   d) to add to my retirement income by working ( ).
   e) to do a lot of work on my home and/or car, like painting,
      carpentering and so forth ( ).
   f) to spend more time on my old hobbies ( ).
   g) to spend time on new hobbies ( ).
   h) other _____
          (please specify)

8. In general, I found that planning for retirement was:

   a) very useful ( ).
   b) somewhat useful ( ).
   c) not very useful ( ).
   d) not useful at all ( ).

9. Before I retired, I received from my company:

   a) a good deal of pre-retirement counseling and guidance ( ).
   b) some counseling and guidance ( ).
   c) very little counseling and guidance ( ).
   d) no counseling and guidance at all ( ).

10. Looking back, I think it would have been better if I had received:

    a) more pre-retirement counseling and guidance ( ).
    b) about the same amount ( ).
    c) less ( ).
    d) none at all--I don't really think it helped ( ).

(3)

11. I received useful information and guidance about retirement from:
(check all that apply)

a) my company's pre-retirement program ( ).
b) friends and relatives ( ).
c) books, magazines, radio and TV ( ).
d) associations of retired persons ( ).
e) I never got any information or guidance that was of use ( ).
f) other_____
       please describe

II. NOW WE WOULD LIKE TO ASK SOME QUESTIONS ABOUT YOUR RETIREMENT EXPERIENCES AND THE PROBLEMS YOU MAY HAVE FACED.

12. Here is a list of common problems encountered by retired people. Please check boxes after all those problems which you have encountered. In addition we would like some idea of which problems you consider to be most serious. Please check the three most serious problems.

Problem	I have encountered this	(check three most serious)
a) inflation and the rising cost of living	( )	( )
b) transportation problems	( )	( )
c) my health	( )	( )
d) my spouse's health	( )	( )
e) housing appropriate for retirement	( )	( )
f) not enough friends or social life	( )	( )
g) not enough to do with my time	( )	( )
h) too much time and effort spent on taking care of home maintenance	( )	( )
i) not enough personal security, worry about personal safety	( )	( )
j) not enough contact with children or other members of family	( )	( )
k) feeling useless because not working	( )	( )
l) other_____ (please describe)	( )	( )

13. Before retirement, I expected that retirement would be:

a) a very pleasant experience ( ).
b) somewhat pleasant, but not entirely ( ).
c) somewhat unpleasant, but with some satisfactions too ( ).
d) an unpleasant experience, with little or no satisfactions ( ).

(4)

14. All things considered, my retirement experience has been:

    a) more satisfactory than I had expected ( ).
    b) about what I expected ( ).
    c) less satisfactory than I had expected ( ).

15. After retirement: (check all that apply)

    a) my health has been better than I expected ( ).
    b) my health has been worse than I expected ( ).
    c) my income has been more than I expected ( ).
    d) my income has been less than I expected ( ).
    e) my social life has been better than I expected ( ).
    f) my social life has been less satisfying than I expected ( ).

16. When I retired, I thought that prices would rise: (check one)

    a) faster than they have risen in the past year ( ).
    b) about as fast as they have risen in the past year ( ).
    c) somewhat, but not as fast as they are now rising ( ).
    d) nowhere near as fast as they are now rising ( ).
    e) I didn't really give it much thought at the time I retired ( ).

17. In the past year, I have had to: (check all that apply)

    a) sell my house ( ).
    b) move to cheaper housing ( ).
    c) get rid of my car ( ).
    d) cut my standard of living ( ).
    e) sell some of my stock ( ).
    f) dip into my savings somewhat ( ).
    g) dip into my savings quite a lot ( ).
    h) none of the above ( ).

18. Looking at the future, I think our standard of living will fall:

    a) a great deal ( ).
    b) somewhat, but not too much ( ).
    c) little or not at all ( ).
    d) it is likely to rise ( ).

(5)

III. NOW WE WOULD LIKE TO ASK YOU SOME QUESTIONS ABOUT YOUR ACTIVITIES
      DURING RETIREMENT.

19. Since my retirement I have worked for pay: (check the box which applies
     to you.)

     a) just about every month ( ).   Answer next
     b) most months ( ).   question.
     c) some months but not very many ( ).
     d) I have not worked for pay at all ( ).
         (If you check this box, then skip to question 39 on page 8).

20. Are you working for pay now? Yes ( ) If yes, skip to question 25)
     ──────────────────────────────── No ( ) If no, answer next question.

21. If you answered No to question 20, have you worked for pay at any
     time during the past 12 months? Yes ( ) If yes, answer next question.
     ──────────────────────────── No ( ) If no, answer question 23.

22. Although I am not working at present, I have worked _____ months
                                                         (how many)
     during the past 12 months ( ). Then skip to question 28 on page 6.

23. I have not worked for pay at any time during the past 12 months because:
     (check all boxes that apply to you)

     a) there are no suitable jobs for people my age ( ).
     b) my health does not permit me to work ( ).
     c) after all the taxes and other deductions, including Social
         Security deductions, it doesn't pay to work ( ).
     d) I don't want to work any more ( ).
     e) other _____ ( ).
              (please specify)

24. Although I have not worked any time during the past 12 months, I
     would: (check all boxes which apply to you)

     a) go back to work if I could find a suitable job, part time ( )
         or full time ( ).
     b) go back to work if my health permits ( ).
     c) work if my social security benefits were not decreased ( ).
     d) go back to work some time in the future if prices continue to
         rise the way they have been rising ( ).
     e) other _____ ( ).
              (please describe)
         Then skip to question 28 on page 6.

25. I have held my present job for _____ months.
                                   (how many)

(6)

26. In my present job, I usually work:
    (check <u>one</u> in column A and <u>one</u> in column B)

A (hours per week)	B (weeks per year)
1. 35 hours a week or more ( )	1. 48 weeks a year or more ( )
2. between 20 and 35 hours ( )	2. between 20 and 48 weeks ( )
3. less than 20 hours a week ( )	3. less than 20 weeks a year ( )

27. If it were up to me, the work schedule I would work would be:
    (check <u>one</u> in column A and <u>one</u> in column B)

A (hours per week)	B (weeks per year)
1. 35 hours a week or more ( )	1. 48 weeks a year or more ( )
2. between 20 and 35 hours ( )	2. between 20 and 48 weeks ( )
3. less than 20 hours a week ( )	3. less than 20 weeks a year ( )

→ 28. Whenever I have worked since retirement, it has been because:
    (check all boxes that apply)

    a) I needed more income ( ).
    b) I was concerned about the effect of inflation upon my future
       income ( ).
    c) I wanted more contact with people ( ).
    d) Taken as a whole, I like working ( ).
    e) Other_____( ).

29. Since retirement, when working for pay, I have usually worked:
    (check <u>one</u> in column A and <u>one</u> in column B)

A (hours per week)	B (weeks per year)
1. 35 hours a week or more ( )	1. 48 weeks a year or more ( )
2. between 20 and 35 hours ( )	2. between 20 and 48 weeks ( )
3. less than 20 hours a week ( )	3. less than 20 weeks a year ( )

30. Since retirement, when I have earned money, I have usually:

    a) been on the payroll of a company ( ).
    b) been self-employed ( ).
    c) done work for a private individual ( ).

31. Since retirement, when I have worked for a company, it usually has had:

    a) less than 50 employees ( ).
    b) between 50 and 250 employees ( ).
    c) between 250 and 1,000 employees ( ).
    d) over 1,000 employees ( ).

(7)

32. Since retirement, when I have worked for pay, my work has usually been:

    a) very much like what I did before I retired ( ).
    b) somewhat like what I did before I retired ( ).
    c) very different from what I did before I retired ( ).
       If you checked this box, please describe briefly what you have
       done _____.

33. Since retirement, when I have worked for pay, my work has usually been:

    a) more satisfying than what I did before retiring ( ).
    b) about the same as far as satisfaction goes ( ).
    c) less satisfying ( ).

34. When I have worked for a company, it has usually been:

    a) a manufacturing company ( ).
    b) a retailing establishment ( ).
    c) a utility ( ).
    d) other_____
             (please describe the main product or service of the company)

35. Since retirement, whenever I have looked for a job I have usually found it:

    a) immediately ( ).
    b) within the month ( ).
    c) between a month and six months ( ).
    d) after looking six months or more ( ).
    e) I gave up looking for work after _____ months because it
       seemed useless to spend any more time looking for one.

36. I have usually got my job(s) through: (check all boxes that apply)

    a) friends or relatives ( ).
    b) contacts I made before I retired ( ).
    c) my former company ( ).
    d) private employment agencies ( ).
    e) the state employment service ( ).
    f) want ads or other advertisements ( ).
    g) apply directly to the employer myself ( ).
    h) other_____.
             (please describe briefly)

(8)

37. My hourly rate of pay in the jobs I have had since retirement has
    <u>usually</u> been about _____ .
                               (dollars)   (cents)

    This is:

    a) less than half what I earned before retiring ( ).
    b) about half what I earned before retiring ( ).
    c) more than 1/2, but less than what I earned before retiring ( ).
    d) about the same ( ).
    e) somewhat more ( ).
    f) a lot more ( ).

38. In the jobs I have had since retirement, I have usually received:

    a) no fringe benefits at all ( ).
    b) much less in the way of fringe benefits than I received before
       retiring ( ).
    c) somewhat less in the way of fringe benefits ( ).
    d) about the same fringe benefits ( ).
    e) more in the way of fringe benefits ( ).

IF YOU HAPPENED TO SKIP QUESTIONS 20 TO 38 BUT HAVE WORKED DURING RETIREMENT,
PLEASE GO BACK TO QUESTION 20.

39. Since I retired, I have had:

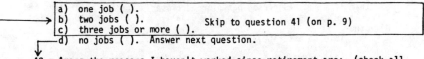

    a) one job ( ).
    b) two jobs ( ).   Skip to question 41 (on p. 9)
    c) three jobs or more ( ).
    d) no jobs ( ). Answer next question.

40. Among the reasons I haven't worked since retirement are: (check all
    that apply)

    a) there are no post-retirement job opportunities in my field ( ).
    b) there are no post-retirement job opportunities in any field ( ).
    c) my health does not permit my working ( ).
    d) after taxes, social security and other deductions, it doesn't pay ( ).
    e) I don't want to work anymore ( ).
    f) I have encountered age discrimination ( ).
    g) I couldn't find a suitable job although I looked for work for
       _____ months.   (how many)
    h) Other _____
             (please describe)

(9)

→ 41. If I continue to work or go back to work in the future, I would
       probably prefer to work: (check <u>one</u> in column A and <u>one</u> in Column B)

     A (hours per week)   B (weeks per year)
1. 3$\overline{5}$ hours a week or more ( )   1. 4$\overline{8}$ weeks a year or more ( )
2. between 20 and 35 hours ( )   2. between 20 and 48 weeks ( )
3. less than 20 hours a week ( )   3. less than 20 weeks a year ( )

42. As far as post-retirement work is concerned, I: (check all that apply)

    a) resent it because I can't find a suitable job ( ).
    b) resent it because I have had to work to earn enough to live on ( ).
    c) resent it because my skills and experience have not been recognized
        properly when I have worked ( ).
    d) have been happy to discover that my skills and experience have
        been appreciated and respected ( ).
    e) have been happy to work because I have been able to do things at
        work which I couldn't do before I retired ( ).
    f) other_____
          (please describe)

43. As far as post-retirement work is concerned, I believe: (check all that
     apply)

    a) that you should be able to work if you want to ( ).
    b) that older workers should move over for younger people and therefore
        should not try to work after they retire ( ).
    c) that if a retired person has planned properly for his retirement and
        what he can do after retiring, he usually will not want to work ( ).
    d) other_____
          (please describe)

44. Here is a list of important activities. We are interested in how much
     time you usually give to these activities in a typical week. Please
     check the box that is most appropriate. For example, if you spend about
     three hours a week in "home maintenance and improvements" check the 1-5
     hours box opposite this activity.

Activity	No time at all	\-\- Usual hours per week \-\- 1-5	5-10	10-15	15-20	over 20
a) Working for pay	( )	( )	( )	( )	( )	( )
b) Volunteer work (for example, church or community work)	( )	( )	( )	( )	( )	( )
c) Hobbies & recreation	( )	( )	( )	( )	( )	( )
d) Routine domestic chores	( )	( )	( )	( )	( )	( )
e) Home maintenance and improvement (painting, carpentry, etc.)	( )	( )	( )	( )	( )	( )

(10)

45. Here is a list of activities that are recreational. We would like to know how often you engaged in these activities before you retired and how often you engage in them now.

		Before I retired			In the past 12 months		
		Often	sometimes	never	Often	sometimes	never
a)	Active sports	( )	( )	( )	( )	( )	( )
b)	Gardening	( )	( )	( )	( )	( )	( )
c)	Travel	( )	( )	( )	( )	( )	( )
d)	Attending sports events, movies, etc.	( )	( )	( )	( )	( )	( )
e)	Television, card games	( )	( )	( )	( )	( )	( )
f)	Hobbies	( )	( )	( )	( )	( )	( )
g)	Adult education courses	( )	( )	( )	( )	( )	( )
h)	Other	( )	( )	( )	( )	( )	( )
	(describe)						

IV. NOW WE WOULD LIKE TO ASK SOME QUESTIONS ABOUT YOU AND YOUR FAMILY.

46. When I retired, I was:

     a) married ( ).
     b) widowed ( ).
     c) divorced or separated ( ).
     d) never married ( ).

47. At the present time, I am:

     a) married ( ).
     b) widowed ( ).
     c) divorced or separated ( ).
     d) never married ( ).

48. Check all the following statements that apply to you:

     a) my spouse was not employed when I retired ( ).
     b) my spouse was employed, but I would have retired in any case ( ).
     c) my spouse was employed and we decided that we should both retire at about the same time ( ).
     d) my spouse kept on working and this helped to make it possible for me to retire ( ).
     e) when I retired, my spouse went back to work ( ).
     f) my spouse delayed retiring because I had to retire ( ).
     g) if my spouse had not been working, I would have retired even sooner. I didn't want to be the only one in the family who was retired ( ).
     h) without our two pensions, neither my spouse nor I could have afforded to retire ( ).
     i) my spouse and I have usually made our decision about working separately and that was the case with the decision to retire ( ).
     j) my spouse has never worked ( ).
     k) other_____

(11)

49. Did you delay your retirement because you still had to support children?

     Yes ( )
     No ( )

50. Did you delay your retirement because you had to contribute to the support of parents or other persons?

     Yes ( )
     No ( )

51. I am male ( ), female ( ).

52. I am white ( ), black ( ), other ( ).

53. I went to school for:

     a) less than eight years ( ).
     b) nine to eleven years ( ) (some high school).
     c) twelve years ( ) (graduated from high school).
     d) 13-15 years ( ) (some college).
     e) 16 years ( ) (graduated from college).
     f) more than 16 years ( ) (postgraduate).

54. In addition to school, I received vocational training: (check all that apply)

     a) in an apprenticeship program ( ).
     b) during military service ( ).
     c) from a vocational school not operated by my company ( ).
     d) from a vocational training facility operated by my company ( ).
     e) none ( ).
     f) other _____
         (please describe)

55. My total family income for the year before I retired, including my own earnings, my spouse's earnings and/or pension, our income from investments or rental property, and all other sources was approximately:

     a) over $30,000 ( ).
     b) between $25,000 and $30,000 ( ).
     c) between $20,000 and $25,000 ( ).
     d) between $15,000 and $20,000 ( ).
     e) between $10,000 and $15,000 ( ).
     f) less than $10,000 ( ).

56. My hourly rate of pay in the year before I retired was _____ _____ .
                                                            ($'s)   (¢'s)

(12)

57. During the past year, my average <u>monthly</u> Social Security benefit check has been about $_____.
      (monthly)

58. During the past year, my average <u>monthly</u> company pension check has been about $_____.
      (monthly)

59. In the past year, my total family income, including what I get from my pension and social security benefits, what I earn from working, what I and my spouse have received in the form of income from investments, interest and rental property, and what my spouse has received from her pensions and from what she has earned by working, has amounted to approximately:

   a) over $30,000 ( ).
   b) between $25,000 and $30,000 ( ).
   c) between $20,000 and $25,000 ( ).
   d) between $15,000 and $20,000 ( ).
   e) between $10,000 and $15,000 ( ).
   f) less than $10,000 ( ).

60. Which of the following statements best applies to you?

   a) I live in the same house or apartment I lived in before I retired ( ).
   b) I have moved since retirement, but still live less than twenty miles away from where I lived before retirement ( ).
   c) I now live more than a thousand miles from where I lived before retirement ( ).
   d) other _____
         (please specify about how many miles you now live from where you lived before retirement)

61. I own a home that is worth about $_____.

62. I still owe about $_____ on the mortgage of my home.

63. Compared to retired people my age that I know of, I would say that my health is:

   a) better ( ).
   b) about the same ( ).
   c) worse ( ).

(13)

64. I would have retired <u>earlier</u> if: (check all that apply)

   a) I had known in advance what retirement would be like ( ).
   b) my company had not offered me either a raise ( ) or a promotion ( )
       if I would delay retiring.
   c) my company had permitted me to make contributions that would have
       increased my pension ( ).
   d) my company had had a policy of recalling retired employees fairly
       often to cover its temporary need for additional workers ( ).
   e) none of the above. I would have retired when I did no matter
       what my company had done ( ).
   f) other _____
               (please specify)

65. I would have retired <u>later</u> if: (check all that apply)

   a) I had known in advance what retirement would be like ( ).
   b) the company offered flexible work schedules ( ) and/or reduced
       hours ( ) for older workers.
   c) the company had offered older workers better chances for promotions ( ),
       and/or raises in wages ( ).
   d) the company had offered older workers job reassignments that reduced
       the pressure of work ( ).
   e) the company had offered older workers better opportunities to receive
       retraining ( ).
   f) the company had required retirement at age 70 rather than age 65 ( ).
   g) the company had impressed more strongly upon all supervisors that
       the company would not tolerate age discrimination against older workers ( ).
   h) none of the above. I would have retired when I did no matter what my
       company had done ( ).
   i) other _____
               (please specify)

V.   NOW WE WOULD LIKE TO GIVE YOU AN OPPORTUNITY TO COMMENT UPON A NUMBER OF
     THINGS IN YOUR OWN WORDS.

Taking everything into account, the two or three <u>best</u> things about retirement
have been:

1)_____
2)_____
3)_____

Taking everything into account, the two or three <u>worst</u> things about retirement
have been:

1)_____
2)_____
3)_____

(14)

What other comments, if any, would you like to make about post-retirement employment opportunities and experiences, including problems of age discrimination?

What comments would you like to make about company pension or retirement policies? About how they have utilized older workers?

What comments would you like to make about national policies with respect to retirement, age discrimination, social security or other policies that affect older people?

If there are other matters, including unusual experiences you have had, or thoughts about retirement that you would like to share with other people who are retired or will soon be retired, or any advice that you would like to give to people who are retired or who have some responsibility for retirement policies and programs that affect older people, we would like to hear from you. Please attach additional sheets if necessary.

APPENDIX B

Percentage Distributions: Single-Response Questions

1.a Company: % of respondents (N=848)
    Utility   33
    Manufacturing   24
    Chain Store   43

1.b Year of retirement (grouped):   % of respondents (N=793)
    A) 1968-1972   36
       1973-1978   64

    B) 1968-1969   10
       1970-1972   26
       1973-1975   32
       1976-1977   20
       1978   12

2.a Age at retirement (grouped):   % of respondents (N=837)
    50-54   5
    55-59   24
    60-61   16
    62   22
    63-64   13
    65   20

2.b Job tenure in years (grouped):   % of respondents (N=838)
    1-9   3
    10-19   17
    20-29   39
    30-39   30
    40 and over   11

3. Job Classification: % of respondents (N=835)
    Technical, clerical, and
    service (3 months training
    required before employment)   6
    High-skill white-collar   2
    High-skill blue-collar   8
    Other skilled and semi-skilled   31
    Low-skill clerical and sales   27
    Low-skill blue-collar   12
    Low-skill service   1
    Managers, administrators, and
    supervisors   15

Note: Numbers of individual items correspond with Retirement
      Activities Study Questionnaire. Responses to each
      question total 100 percent.

4. See Appendix C for frequency distributions by respondents and by response for all multi-response questions.

5. Retirement timing: % of respondents (N=796)
   At about right time   80
   Too soon   18
   Too late   2

6. How long in advance of
   retirement respondent knew
   when it would occur: % of respondents (N=827)
   More than three years   25
   One to three years   24
   Three months to one year   26
   Less than three months but
     knew date of retirement   12
   Did not know in advance   14

7. See Appendix C.

8. Usefulness of planning: % of respondents (N=744)
   Very useful   46
   Somewhat useful   34
   Not very useful   11
   Not of any use at all   9

9. Amount of counseling
   received from company: % of respondents (N=808)
   A good deal   17
   Some   30
   Very little   18
   None   35

10. Amount of counseling that
    would have been desirable: % of respondents (N=710)
    More counseling   32
    About the same   42
    Less   0
    None   25

11. See Appendix C.

12. See Appendix C.

13. Expectations that retirement
    experience would be: % of respondents (N=823)
    Very pleasant   66
    Somewhat pleasant   28
    Somewhat unpleasant   5
    Very unpleasant   2

14. Experience compared
     to expectations: % of respondents (N=820)
       More satisfactory   31
       About as expected   54
       Less satisfactory   15

15.a Health compared with
     expectations: % of respondents (N=669)
       Better   70
       Worse   30

15.b Income compared with
     expectations: % of respondents (N=606)
       More   41
       Less   59

15.c Social life compared
     with expectations: % of respondents (N=608)
       Better   67
       Worse   33

16. Expectations of
     inflation compared
     with actual inflation: % of respondents (N=833)
       Faster   3
       About as fast   5
       Somewhat but not as fast   27
       Nowhere near as fast   42
       Did not give it much thought   24

17. See Appendix C.

18. Standard of living will: % of respondents (N=821)
       Fall a lot   31
       Fall somewhat   42
       Not change very much   17
       Possibly rise   11

19. Work experience
     during retirement: % of respondents (N=840)
       Almost every month   7
       Most months   5
       Not many months   12
       None   76

20. and 21. When employed
    during retirement: % of respondents (N=899)
       At time of survey   13
       Not employed at time of
       survey but at some time
       in previous 12 months   4
       Employed during retirement
       but not in past 12 months   7
       Not employed during
       retirement   76

22.   Months worked in past
       year (grouped):   % of respondents (N=35)
       Three months or less   46
       Four months to six months   37
       More than six months   17

    (<u>Note</u>: N includes only those respondents not at work at
              time of survey but with work experience in
              previous 12 months.)

23.   See Appendix C.

24.   See Appendix C.

25.   Months employed in job held
       at time of survey (grouped):   % of respondents (N=99)
       1 to 19 months   38
       20 to 39 months   28
       40 to 59 months   11
       60 to 79 months   12
       80 to 99 months   10

26.   Work schedules of respondents
       employed at time of survey: % of respondents (N=179)
       A) Hours per week
          35 or more   27
          20 to 35   46
          20 or less   27

       B) Weeks per year   % of respondents (N=161)
          48 or more   45
          20 to 48   46
          20 or less   9

27. Preferred work schedule
     of respondents employed
     at time of survey: % of respondents (N=105)
     A) Hours per week
          35 or more   21
          20 to 35   50
          20 or less   29

     B) Weeks per year   % of respondents (N=161)
          48 or more   36
          20 to 48   50
          20 or less   14

28. See Appendix C.

29. Usual work schedules of
     respondents who have worked
     during retirement: % of respondents (N=179)
     A) Hour per week
          35 or more   27
          20 to 35   46
          20 or less   27

     B) Weeks per year   % of respondents (N=161)
          48 or more   34
          20 to 48   39
          20 or less   27

                                % of respondents who worked at any
30. Employed by: time during retirement (N=186)
     Company   60
     Self-employed   16
     Private individual   18
     Company and self-employed   3
     Self-employed and private
      individual   3
     All three types of employment   1

31. Size of employing   % of respondents who worked at any
     company: time during retirement (N=147)
     Less than 50 employees   56
     Between 50 and 250 employees   22
     Between 250 and 1,000 employees   12
     More than 1,000 employees   11

32. Similarity of post-
     retirement work to   % of respondents who worked at any
     preretirement job: time during retirement (N=191)
     Very similar   16
     Somewhat like   19
     Very different   65

33. Satisfaction of post-   % of respondents who had work
     retirement work compared   experience during retirement
     with preretirement job: (N=189)
     More satisfying   33
     About as satisfying   46
     Less satisfying   22

34. Type of company   % of respondents who worked
     usually worked   for a company during retirement
     for: (N=153)
     Manufacturing   10
     Retail   44
     Utility   6
     Other   39

35. How long did it take to   % of respondents who searched
     obtain postretirement job: for employment (N=138)
     Obtained immediately   49
     Within a month   22
     From one to six months   10
     Six months or longer   7
     Unsuccessful search of
       one to three months   2
       four to six months   1
       more than six months   2
     No search: job was offered   6

36. See Appendix C.

37.a Hourly wage rate in
     postretirement jobs   % of respondents with post-
     (grouped):   retirement employment (N=112)
     Less than $3.00   10
     $3.00 to $3.99   42
     $4.00 to $4.99   17
     $5.00 to $6.99   15
     $7.00 to $9.99   10
     $10.00 or more   6

37.b Postretirement wage   (N=181)
     compared to preretire-
     ment wage:
     Less than half   48
     About half   13
     More than half but less
       than preretirement wage   17
     About the same   9
     Somewhat more   9
     A lot more   3

38. Postretirement fringe
     benefits compared to   % of respondents compared to
     preretirement: preretirement (N=   )
       None   71
       Much less   16
       Somewhat less   5
       About the same   6
       More   3

39. Number of jobs since
     retirement: % of respondents (N=837)
       One   14
       Two   5
       Three or more   4
       Self-employed or farmer   1
       No jobs   77

40. See Appendix C.

41. Preferred work schedule if
     respondent goes back to
     work or continues to work: % of respondents (N=473)
     A. Hours per week
           35 or more   7
           20 to 35   36
           20 or less   57

     B. Weeks per year
           48 or more   11
           20 to 48   40
           20 or less   49

42. See Appendix C.

43. See Appendix C.

44. Time spent in
     major activities   % distribution of respondents

Activity	No time	1-5	5-10	10-15	15-20	Over 20
Working for pay (N=473)	77	3	1	2	5	13
Volunteer work (N=499)	39	43	10	4	1	3
Hobbies & recreation (N=629)	5	30	25	16	12	13
Domestic chores (N=699)	3	32	21	16	10	19
Home maintenance (N=566)	15	44	21	10	4	6

45. Frequency of recreational activities:

Activity	Before retirement			In past 12 months		
	Often	Some-times	Never	Often	Some-times	Never
Active sports	20	43	38	20	34	46
		(N=522)			(N=505)	
Gardening	40	40	20	48	34	18
		(N=652)			(N=629)	
Travel	24	70	6	30	59	11
		(N=683)			(N=663)	
Sports events	13	67	20	13	58	29
		(N=589)			(N=556)	
Television, card games, etc.	48	49	3	60	38	1
		(N=721)			(N=710)	
Hobbies	8	56	17	47	41	12
		(N=606)			(N=609)	
Adult education	6	33	61	7	27	66
		(N=484)			(N=470)	

% distribution of respondents

46. Marital status before retirement: % of respondents (N=835)

Married	76
Widowed	12
Divorced or separated	6
Never married	7

47. Marital status at time of survey: % of respondents (N=836)

Married	69
Widowed	18
Divorced or separated	6
Never married	7

48. See Appendix C.

49. Four percent of respondents delayed retirement to support children.

50. Three percent of respondents delayed retirement to support others.

51. Gender: % of respondents (N=841)

Male	54
Female	46

52. Ethnic divisions: % of respondents (N=839)
      White   99
      Black   1
      Other   0.2

53. Education: % of respondents (N=842)
      Eight years or less   10
      Nine to 11 years   32
      12 years   38
      13 to 15 years   17
      16 years   2
      More than 16   1

54. See Appendix C.

55. Total family income before
     retirement (in 1979 $):   % of respondents (N=732)
      $30,000 or more   19
      $25,000 to $30,000   13
      $20,000 to $25,000   23
      $15,000 to $20,000   18
      $10,000 to $15,000   21
      $10,000 or less   6

56. Hourly pay in year before
     retirement (in 1979 $):   % of respondents (N=556)
      Below $5.00   10
      $5.00 to $7.49   45
      $7.50 to $9.99   30
      $10.00 to $12.49   11
      $12.50 to $14.99   3
      $15.00 or more   1

57. Average monthly Social
     Security benefit: % of respondents (N=694)
      $1.00 to $199   1
      $200 to $299   19
      $300 to $399   54
      $400 to $499   23
      $500 or more   4

58. Average monthly company
     pension benefit: % of respondents (N=532)
      $1.00 to $99   10
      $100 to $199   19
      $200 to $299   28
      $300 to $399   23
      $400 to $499   12
      $500 or $599   5
      $600 or more   3

59. Total family income in year
     before survey (1979):   % of respondents (N=772)
       $30,000 or more   2
       $25,000 to $30,000   4
       $20,000 to $25,000   6
       $15,000 to $20,000   12
       $10,000 to $15,000   32
       $10,000 or less   45

60. Residential mobility since
     retirement, live in: % of respondents (N=830)
       Same house   68
       Less than 20 miles away   11
       Between 20 and 1,000 miles   16
       More than 1,000 miles   4

61. Value of home: % of respondents (N=652)
       Less than $20,000   9
       $20,000 to $29,000   14
       $30,000 to $39,000   21
       $40,000 to $49,000   18
       $50,000 to $59,000   13
       $60,000 to $69,000   11
       $70,000 to $79,000   5
       $80,000 or more   8

62. Mortgage outstanding
     on home: % of respondents (N=425)
       None   72
       $1,000 to $9,000   16
       $10,000 to $19,000   7
       $20,000 to $29,000   3
       $30,000 to $40,000   2

63. Own health compared
     to associates: % of respondents (N=831)
       Better   39
       About the same   49
       Worse   12

64. See Appendix C.

65. See Appendix C.

APPENDIX C

Percentage Distributions: Multi-Response Questions

4.	Reason retired:	Count	% of responses	% of cases
	Could afford to	283	14	34
	Health-necessary	155	8	18
	Health-desirable	102	5	12
	Pressure	204	10	24
	Treatment by management	100	5	12
	Treatment by supervisors	77	4	9
	Treatment by other employees	26	1	3
	Did not pay to work	85	4	10
	Mandatory retirement	203	10	24
	Worked long enough	281	14	33
	Attractive pension offer	68	3	8
	Social Security disability benefits	87	4	10
	Company disability benefits	65	3	8
	Retirement suggested by supervisor	48	2	6
	Was laid off	13	1	2
	Other reasons	228	11	27
	Total	2,025	100	239
	3 missing cases		846 valid cases	

7.	Planning for retirement:	Count	% of responses	% of cases
	Where to live	265	14	33
	To move	137	7	17
	How to spend time	309	16	39
	To work	106	6	13
	Home maintenance	273	14	34
	Old hobbies	325	17	41
	New hobbies	204	11	26
	Other planning	273	14	34
	Total	1,892	100	238
	54 missing cases		795 valid cases	

11.	Sources of useful information about retirement:	Count	% of responses	% of cases
	Company	337	31	43
	Friends & relatives	160	15	20
	Books, magazines, et al.	160	15	20
	Retirement associations	141	13	18
	Had no sources	212	19	27
	Other sources	82	8	11
	Total	1,092	100	140
	66 missing cases		783 valid cases	

12.a Less serious problems encountered during retirement:

	Count	% of responses	% of cases
Inflation	186	21	38
Transporation	69	8	14
Own health	83	9	17
Spouse's health	65	7	13
Housing	37	4	8
Lack of friends	61	7	12
Not enough to do	43	5	9
Too much time on home maintenance	75	8	15
Personal security	58	7	12
Lack of contact with family	54	6	11
Feeling useless	60	7	12
Other problems	100	11	20
Total	891	100	181

357 missing cases   492 valid cases

12.b Three more serious problems encountered during retirement:

	Count	% of responses	% of cases
Inflation	579	37	91
Transporation	109	7	17
Own health	237	15	37
Spouse's health	180	11	28
Housing	44	3	7
Lack of friends	42	3	7
Not enough to do	62	4	10
Too much time on home maintenance	75	5	12
Personal security	101	6	16
Lack of contact with family	43	3	7
Feeling useless	63	4	10
Other problems	42	3	7
Total	1,577	100	247

210 missing cases   639 valid cases

17.

Responses in past year to economic pressure:	Count	% of responses	% of cases
Had to sell house	23	2	3
Had to move to cheaper housing	30	3	4
Had to get rid of car	24	2	3
Had to cut standard of living	249	22	30
Had to sell some stock	99	9	12
Had to dip into savings somewhat	292	26	36
Had to dip into savings a lot	100	9	12
None of the above	327	29	40
Total	1,144	100	140

30 missing cases   819 valid cases

23.

Reasons not employed in past year:	Count	% of responses	% of cases
No suitable job	9	13	16
Health	20	29	35
Does not pay	10	15	17
Don't want to	15	22	26
Other	15	22	26
Total	69	100	119

58 valid cases (asked only of respondents who reported work experience in retirement, but not in the 12 months preceding the survey)

24.

Would consider work in future if:	Count	% of responses	% of cases
Suitable job becomes available	16	21	31
Health permits	15	20	29
No Social Security benefits are lost	7	9	14
There is more inflation	26	34	51
Other	13	17	26
Total	77	100	151

51 valid cases (asked only of respondents who reported work experience in retirement, but not in the 12 months preceding the survey)

28. Reasons for working during retirement:

	Count	% of responses	% of cases
More income	114	27	59
Inflation	69	16	36
Contact with people	81	19	42
Like working	136	32	71
Other	31	7	16
Total	431	100	223

193 valid cases (asked only of respondents who reported work experience during retirement)

36. How obtained jobs during retirement:

	Count	% of responses	% of cases
Through friends and relatives	67	29	37
Through contacts	33	14	18
Through former company	8	4	4
Through private employment agency	6	3	3
Through state employment agency	6	3	3
Through advertisements	34	15	19
Through direct application to employer	57	25	32
Through other means	18	8	10
Total	229	100	127

181 valid cases (asked only of respondents who reported working for an employer during retirement)

40. Reasons for not working during retirement:

	Count	% of responses	% of cases
No jobs in field	51	7	9
No jobs in any field	8	1	1
Health	167	21	29
Does not pay to work	153	19	27
Do not want to work	305	39	53
Age discrimination	26	3	5
Other	78	10	14
Total	788	100	137

576 valid cases (asked only of respondents who reported no work experience during retirement)

42. Attitudes towards
    postretirement work:

	Count	% of responses	% of cases
Resent that no suitable job is available	21	5	7
Resent having to work	39	10	13
Resent nonrecognition of abilities and experience	26	6	8
Glad to be appreciated in postretirement jobs	136	33	44
Happy to work at new things	97	24	31
Other attitudes	89	22	28
Total	408	100	130

313 valid cases

43. General beliefs about
    postretirement work:

	Count	% of responses	% of cases
Retirees should be able to work	563	52	76
Retirees should make room for younger workers	129	12	17
If good planning before retirement, retirees will not want to work	340	31	46
Other beliefs	57	5	8
Total	1,089	100	147

109 missing cases   740 valid cases

44. Hours spent in activities
    in typical week:

	Count	% of responses	% of cases
Work	110	5	14
Volunteer work	306	14	39
Hobbies and recreation	600	28	76
Domestic chores	679	31	87
Home maintenance	481	22	61
Total	2,176	100	277

64 missing cases   785 valid cases

Response to question meant that respondent spent some time in activity.

48. Spouse's work status:	Count	% of responses	% of cases
Spouse not employed at retirement	355	29	56
Spouse employed at retirement	175	14	28
Respondent and spouse retired together	98	8	15
Spouse continued to work	98	8	15
Spouse went back to work	11	1	2
Spouse delayed retirement	21	2	3
Spouse did not want to be only retiree	5	0	1
Needed both pensions to retire	146	12	23
Made separate decisions	104	9	16
Spouse never worked	111	9	18
Other spouse work status	93	8	15
Total	1,217	100	192

214 missing cases   635 valid cases

54. Vocational training:	Count	% of responses	% of cases
Apprenticeship	92	12	17
Training in military service	102	13	18
Training in school not operated by company	136	18	23
Training in school operated by company	136	18	23
No vocational training	171	22	30
Other vocational training	130	17	22
Total	767	100	132

269 missing cases   580 valid cases

64.

Respondent would have retired earlier if:	Count	% of responses	% of cases
Had known what retirement was like	55	8	9
Company had not offered raise or promotion	6	1	1
Company had permitted respondent to make contributions that would have increased pension	66	9	10
Company had policy of recalling retirees fairly often when it had temporary need for them	41	6	6
Would not have retired earlier under any of above conditions	458	63	72
Would have retired earlier under other conditions	97	12	15
Total	723	100	113

211 missing cases   638 valid cases

65.

Respondent would have retired later if:	Count	% of responses	% of cases
Had known what retirement was like	39	5	6
Company had offered flexible or reduced hours	10	1	2
Company had offered better chances for promotions or raises to older workers	24	3	4
Company had offered job reassignments to older workers	94	12	15
Company had offered better opportunities for retraining	25	3	4
Mandatory retirement had been at age 70	101	13	16
Company had stronger policies against age discrimination	55	7	9
Would not have retired later under any of these conditions	373	48	60
Would have retired later under other conditions	62	8	10
Total	783	100	125

223 missing cases   626 valid cases

APPENDIX D
Selected Cross-Tabulations

Table D1. Cross-Tabulation of Major Reasons for Retirement by Major Reasons for Retirement (in percentages)

Major reasons for retirement	Major reasons for retirement					
	Could afford to	Health	Pressure or treatment	Mandatory	Disability benefits	Worked long enough
Could afford to	100	21	36	15	9	57
Health	24	100	37	8	40	23
Pressure or treatment	40	36	100	9	12	43
Mandatory	21	9	11	100	7	19
Disability benefits	23	86	26	12	100	22
Worked long enough	57	20	40	14	9	100

Note: Percentages are based on respondents (N=849) and given for rows only. The percentage total for any row can add up to more than 200 percent because respondents were free to give more than one reason for retirement.

Table D2. Cross-Tabulation of Major Planning Activities for
           Retirement by Major Planning Activities for
           Retirement (in percentages) (N=708)

Major planning activities for retirement	Where to live	How to spend time	To work during retirement
Where to live	100.0	75.0	13.0
How to spend time	37.0	100.0	11.2
To work during retirement	36.8	64.2	100.0

Table D3. Cross-Tabulation of Major Problems Encountered During Retirement by Major Problems Encountered During Retirement (in percentages) (N=815)

Major problems encountered during retirement	Inflation	Trans-portation	Own health	Spouse's health	Lack of friends and/ or contact with family	Not enough to do and/ or feeling useless
Inflation	100.0	21.8	38.3	29.3	17.4	15.2
Transportation	93.8	100.0	43.8	29.2	21.9	10.1
Own health	91.6	24.4	100.0	35.3	20.6	16.6
Spouse's health	91.4	21.2	46.1	100.0	17.1	13.1
Lack of friends and/or contact with family	92.4	27.1	45.8	29.2	100.0	22.2
Not enough to do and/or feeling useless	93.5	14.5	42.7	25.8	25.8	100.0

Table D4. Cross-Tabulation of Reasons for Not Working During Retirement by Reasons for Not Working (in percentages) (N=551)

Reason for not working during retirement	No suitable jobs available	Health	It does not pay	Do not want to work	Encountered age discrimination	Unsuccessful job search	Other reasons
No suitable jobs available	100.0	13.7	27.5	27.5	11.8	5.9	7.8
Health	4.3	100.0	11.2	27.3	1.2	1.2	8.7
It does not pay	9.4	12.1	100.0	47.7	6.7	0.7	7.4
Do not want to work	4.8	15.0	24.2	100.0	0.3	0.0	7.2
Encountered age discrimination	27.3	9.1	45.5	4.5	100.0	18.2	9.1
Unsuccessful job search	33.3	22.2	11.1	0.0	44.4	100.0	22.2
Other reasons	5.6	19.7	15.5	29.6	2.8	2.8	100.0

Table D5. Cross-Tabulation of Extent of Postretirement Work Experience by When Postretirement Work Experience Took Place (in percentages) (N=191)

Extent of postretire- ment work experience	Employed at time of survey	Employed in 12 months pre- ceding survey but at time of survey	Employed during retirement but not at time of survey nor during 12 months preceding survey
Almost every month	94.8	1.7	3.4
Most months	76.9	7.7	15.4
Not many months	24.5	27.7	47.9

APPENDIX E

Statistical Models of the Retirement Decision and the Decision to Work in Retirement

Our analysis has as its central focus two decisions made by the respondents: the decision to take early retirement, and the decision to return to work after retirement.

The information obtained from the survey instrument, including demographic and income data, aspects of the preretirement work history, attitudes toward work, and patterns of postretirement activities, was analyzed to establish to what extent such factors were associated with these two decisions. This information, as was indicated earlier, was obtained from a mail questionnaire to a random sample of retired nonsupervisory personnel of three large corporations, stratified so that the year of retirement was distributed equally for each year from 1968 to 1978 and with one-fifth of the members of the sample having been mandatorily retired, the other four-fifths having elected early retirement.

Investigation of the relationship between these different variables and the decision to take early retirement or to return to work after retirement was conducted largely through cross-tabulation of the data, i.e., the use of contingency tables (defined as a joint frequency distribution of cases according to two or more classificatory variables).*

Cross-tabulation provides at one and the same time a simple but powerful method for determining associations among the variables. Use of two-variable or two-way tables, however, involves the risk of misinterpretation, since one of the two variables may be interactive with others that may actually play a more central role in the relationship. It becomes necessary then to either "control" for such variables or to introduce them explicitly, as was done, for example, with the factors of sex and company affiliation in the case of our analysis.

While in theory a large number of variables may be introduced into cross-tabulation analysis, the sharp reduction in cell frequencies that results from this procedure places severe limits upon such an approach in practice. Regression analysis, on the other hand, not only has the technical capacity to overcome this limitation, but has the additional utility of providing numerical estimates of the degree of relationship among the variables.†

I. Model of the Early Retirement Decision

Cross-tabulation analysis indicated that the decision to take early retirement, when partitioned on sex lines, was based upon the following reasons, in order of priority:

Males
• Health made it necessary or desirable to retire
• Could afford to retire
• Worked long enough
• Treatment of older workers by managers and supervisors
• Pressure of the work
• Receipt of disability benefits
Females
• Worked long enough
• Could afford to retire

---

*Computer analysis was performed through the system of computer programs known as *Statistical Package for the Social Sciences* (SPSS) 2nd ed. (New York: McGraw-Hill) 1975.

†The method of multiple stepwise regression was employed in our analysis. This statistical technique introduces the various independent variables in sequence or steps, with the order of introduction determined by a number of criteria. It becomes possible, after determining what each variable contributes to the association, to remove those with limited explanatory power (see SPSS, op. cit., pp. 338-47).

- Treatment of older workers by managers and supervisors
- Health made it necessary or desirable to retire
- Pressure of the work

In addition, for the women the spouse's employment status was seen to play a significant role in the retirement decision. In the case of the men, most of whom had wives who were not working at the time of their retirement, this was not a major factor.

The early retirement regression model, run separately by sex, had the following variables:

I. Dependent variable (Y). Age at retirement
   Excluding those mandatorily retired, age at retirement was treated as a continuous variable, ranging from ages 50 to 64.
II. Independent variables (X), as of time of retirement.
   A. Demographic
      Marital status: Married, widowed, divorced, separated, never married*
      Education: number of years
      Vocational training: yes/no
   B. Subjective Factors
      Health: necessary or desirable
      Pressures and treatment of older workers
      Could afford to retire
      Worked long enough
   C. Objective Factors
      Company affiliation
      Year retired
      Disability benefits obtainable (yes/no)
      Wage rate (adjusted)
      Family income (adjusted)
      Years worked for company
      Job title
      Postretirement benefits
      Value of house
      Spouse's work status (for those with spouse)
   D. Expectational Factors†
      Planned: to work; use of time; all other plans

---

*Omitted for the men since so many (86%) checked "married."
†No problem was encountered by the fact that some of the variables were continuous and others dichotomous.

Retirement Expectations: very pleasant; somewhat pleasant;
somewhat unpleasant; very unpleasant
Inflation Expectations: anticipated; not anticipated

For the women, the variables indicated by regression analysis as
having the largest effect on the age at which retirement took place
were, in descending order:
   spouses' employment status at time of retirement (>)*
   availability of disability benefits (>)
   year of retirement
   job title "low-skill clerical and sales" (>)
   planned to work after retirement (>)
   any vocational training
   being widowed
   amount formal education (>)
   adjusted preretirement hourly pay
Together, these with a handful of considerably less important
variables "explained" 44 percent of the variance in age at retirement of the women.†
   In sum, women retired at an earlier age if
   1. their husbands were employed at the time
   2. they were entitled to disability benefits
   3. they were in the low-skill clerical and sales job class
   4. they planned to work after retirement anyway
   5. they had more formal education
Utility women, who retired at a younger age than other women,
fitted into categories (1), (3), and (5).
On the other hand, women retired at a later age not only if these
conditions were not present, but if they were widowed (the pressures to continue work in this case are obvious) and if their adjusted hourly pay was higher rather than lower (the inducements
here are equally obvious). The year of retirement, which is posi-
tively associated with (older) age at retirement, seems a surrogate
for years worked for the company, which is obviously related to the
age of retirement.
   In the case of the men, the important variables were years
worked for the company; health (>); receipt of disability benefits
(>); having the job title high-skill blue-collar. These, with a few

---

*Minus signs indicate a negative relationship, viz., spouse's employment was asso-
ciated with a *younger* age at retirement.
†See Appendix E for summary tables of the regression analyses.

other variables of rapidly dwindling numerical importance "explained" 30 percent of the decisions when to take early retirement. The positive association between "years worked for the company" and age at retirement has already been discussed in the case of the women. The fact that one's health makes it necessary or desirable to retire obviously induces retirement at a younger age, and the receipt of disability benefits makes this decision financially possible. Being in the high-skill blue-collar job category seems to reflect high hourly pay, which, as was seen in the case of the women, is an inducement to defer retirement.

II. Models of the Decision to Work in Retirement

The second set of models deals with the decision to return to work after retirement, which was made by about one in four of the respondents. Two populations were analyzed: those who had worked at all since retirement, and the subset of this population who were the continuous workers, those who worked "almost every month" or "most months since retirement." These coincided largely with those who were employed at the time of the survey or had been employed in the past year.

A. THOSE WHO WORKED AT ALL SINCE RETIREMENT

The dependent variable in this model was "employed since retirement" and the population of the sample now included those who had been mandatorily retired as well as those who elected early retirement. The independent variables were the same as in the retirement decision model, supplemented by the following:

Demographic factors: age at retirement
Objective factors: spouse's work status at retirement
   deleted
Beliefs: believe that older workers should be able to work
   : would have retired later
Problems encountered in retirement
Health better (worse) than anticipated

For the men, the decision to work after retirement was influenced by the following factors, given in descending order of importance:
   planned to work; believes that older workers should have the
      right to work

health was worse than anticipated (>)
value of home
"worked long enough" given as a reason for retirement
family income before retirement (>)

These together "explained" about half the decisions to work after retirement.

The major determinant of the return to work was the prior planning on the part of the work returner, fortified by his belief that older workers have the right to work. Prior analysis had indicated that the *reasons* for planning to return to work were as much social as economic. The positive association between "worked long enough" as a reason for retirement and the return to work can be explained in a variety of ways: the unexpected social void left by not working, the ability to find work which gave more satisfaction than preretirement work, etc. The positive association between "value of home" and the work decision is probably due to the fact that "value of home" is what can be called a confounding variable, linked to other, more determining variables. Those with the most valuable homes were Chain Store employees and these were work returners in large numbers for reasons largely unrelated to the value of their homes.

For the women, a longer list of factors were operative in their decision to work after retirement, factors which explained about 60 percent of these decisions.

As for the men, "planned to work" led the list, followed by disappointed retirement expectations and underestimation of inflation. There was a long list of negative factors militating against the return to work. These included greater formal education, the job titles "low-skill clerical and sales" and "low-skill blue-collar," the size of total benefits; citing pressure or treatment of older workers as a reason for retirement; health found to be worse than anticipated; never married. The first two of these negative factors reflect the low work return rate of Utility women just as the low-skill blue-collar and "never married" factors are dominated by the low work rate of Manufacturer women.

B. THE CONTINUOUS WORKERS

The regression model was modified so that the dependent variable became "employed past year and now" to include those currently employed at the time of the survey or worked in the past year. The independent variables were modified as follows:

Demographic: current marital status replaces marital status before retirement; present age replaces age at retirement

Expectational factors: planned to work, inflation expectations deleted, expectations about the future standard of living added

Problems: responses to economic pressures added

Belief that older workers should have the right to work if they wish was the single most important factor associated with the male members of this group. The subjective belief that their health was better, when compared with others their age, came next. Negative factors included "health made it necessary or desirable" as a reason for retirement and mandatory retirement. These factors were associated with 30 percent of the male continuous work activity.

For the female members of the continuous worker group, the positive factor leading the list was "would have retired later," followed by several negative factors: large total benefits; health given as a reason for retirement; health worse than expected. Together, these variables were associated with 41 percent of the continuous work activity of the women.

For neither sex did "response to economic pressure" or "expectations about the standard of living" play a major role in these decisions to work fairly constantly after retirement. This fact is consistent with the prior cross-tabulation analysis that indicated there were—as yet—few "large" responses to economic pressures.

The regresssion analysis led to the pinpointing of certain variables operative in both the retirement decision and the decision to return to work, either at all or on a continuous basis. While more sophisticated variants of regression analysis might have yielded somewhat more information, it is our belief that the complexities of these decisions cannot be caught readily. The mix of subjective and objective factors and the interactive character of so many of the variables makes us more than normally cautious in imputing causality. Ordinary survey techniques in our view can capture only a limited number of the influences at work. We have been particularly impressed by the idiosyncratic character of the retirement experience.

The associations among variables which came through the sieve of cross-tabulation, combined with the additional focus provided by regression analysis and the comments of the respondents, has led us to a set of conclusions that no one single statistical technique in and of itself can be expected to yield.

Index

ADEA. *See* Age Discrimination in Employment Act
Age Discrimination in Employment Act (ADEA), 139, 144–45
Aging: perceptions of, 13–14; reflections about, 79–80
Aging in America, Trials and Triumphs, 70n

Birth rates, 13
Blue-collar workers, 29

Company: affiliation with, 85–86; loyalty to, 140; and older worker utilization, 138–42
Counseling, 27

Disability benefits, 45
Disengagement, 9, 13
Domestic chores, 8, 60–62; by MPT respondents, 130

Early Retirement: Boon or Bane?, xi, 1, 14n
Education, 84–85
Employment. *See* Postretirement work
Expectations, at retirement, 23–25, 28–33, 124

Health care, 66
Health status, 18, 69–72; and expectations, 30; and fear, 80; of men, 91; and postretirement work, 6, 9, 45, 46,; and questionnaire response, 101; and recreation, 56, 58; research into, 146; and retirement age, 113; as retirement problem, 135; of spouse, 69–70
Hobbies, 55–60; of MPT respondents, 130; time spent in, 57 *table*
Home maintenance, 60–62; as social problem, 72
Human capital, 141

Income, 64–69; family, 89–90; and recreation, 58–59; and retirement expectations, 23–24
Inflation, 5, 50, 64, 66, 124; anticipation of, 102; and postretirement work, 32–33, 49; problems with, 135; response to, 67

Job classification, 2 *table*

Labor force participation rates, 11 *table*; and Social Security, 12

Marital status, 82–83; and expectations, 31

Occupational distribution, 86–87
Older workers: dismissal of, 139; job reassignment for, 140; training programs for, 145; treatment of, 18

Pension: differential costs in, 138; to induce retirement, 122; public 133
Planning, 64, for postretirement work, 145; for retirement, 4–5, 25–28, 95–96, 135
Postretirement work, 5–10, 31 *table*, 96–97; by age group, 115–18; consulting, 122–24; decision for, 34–37; and employer type, 38–44; feelings about, 51–52; fringe benefits, 43; and health status, 70; and inflation, 67–68; job search, 37–38; and mandatory retirement, 109–10; models of, 188–90; of MPT respondents, 125–28; noneconomic motives for, 41; planning for, 26; problems with, 136–37; reasons for, 35 *table*; reservation wage, 147; schedules, 40–41; social contacts in, 127; and social values, 36; and spouse's status, 95–96; stopping, 44–47; wage rates for, 41–43, 46–47, 88

Questionnaire, 148–61; crosstabulations, 179–83; responses to, 162–78

Recreation, 8, 55–60; of MPT respondents, 130; time spent in, 57 *table*
Research, additional areas of, 146–47
Respondents: managerial/professional/technical (MPT), 121–22, 126; nonsupervisory (NS), 1–3, 82–90, 121–22

Retirement: activities study, 14–16; age at, xii, 10, 83–84, 109, 110–18; and company policies, 137; decision, 21–23, 122–25, 136–37, 185–88; early, 131–32, 134–37, 142–46; expectations, 23–25, 28–33, 124; foreknowledge of, 21–22; historical setting, 10–13; mandatory, 17, 18, 20, 109–10, 137; national policies on, 133; nonwork activities during, 128–30; phased, 141; as pleasant experience, 75–76; problems, 5, 65 *table*, 74 *table*, 103 *table*; reasons for, 3–5, 17–20, 90–94; satisfaction with, 57, 63–64; timing of, 76–77, 78 *table*, 79; voluntary, 109–10

Sex-discrimination, 143–44
Social problems, 72–76
Social Security: earnings penalty, 7, 49; policies, 143; and retirement age, xiii, 11, 114–15; and sex discrimination, 144
Survey, response rate, 15

Unions, 132–33

Vintages: age distribution of, 104, 105 *table*; defined, 100–101; expectations of, 102–3; family income of, 107; health status of, 107; and inflation, 104; postretirement work, 104–7
Volunteer work, 8, 53–55; and health status, 70–71; by MPT respondents, 129

Welfare, and retirement income, 66
Women: income of, xiii; recreational patterns of, 59; retirement decisions of, 97–98; retirement income of, 66; in retirement surveys, 120–21; and volunteer work, 54; wage rates of, 87–89
Work. *See* Postretirement work